Cidermaster of Rio Oscuro

Cidermaster
of Rio Oscuro

Harvey Frauenglass

THE UNIVERSITY OF UTAH PRESS

SALT LAKE CITY

Printed on acid-free paper

06 05 04 03 02 01 00

5 4 3 2 1

The events in this book are factual. Names of certain people and places have been changed in the interest of privacy.

Excerpt from "The Study of Ice" from *The Spirit That Wants Me: A New Mexico Anthology*, edited by Diane Duff, Jill Kiefer, and Michelle Miller (Albuquerque: Duff, Inc., 1991). Reprinted by permission of Duff, Inc.

An earlier version of "In the Attic, in the Darkness," by Charles E. Cockelreas appeared in *Talking from the Heart*, edited by David Johnson and Charles E. Cockelreas (Albuquerque: Men's Network Press, 1990). Reprinted by permission of Men's Network Press.

Library of Congress Cataloging-in-Publication Data

Frauenglass, Harvey, 1929–

Cidermaster of Rio Oscuro / Harvey Frauenglass.

p. cm.

ISBN 0-87480-660-7 (alk. paper)

1. Farm life—New Mexico—Rio Oscuro Region. 2. Frauenglass, Harvey, 1929– I. Title.

S521.5.N6 F73 2000

634'.11'092—dc21

00-008268

FOR GAYLE

and for the children and grandchildren
of our blended families

Mark, Jacque, Peter, and Jani
Connie
Andrew
Peter and Trevor
Rick
Jamie and Jessica
Susan

and for Marni Hannelore
in loving memory

Contents

Acknowledgments

COUNTLESS people, friends and family and strangers, past and present, have helped enlarge and enrich our lives on the farm and thus make this book possible. I have mentioned many in the text by name; in the few cases where names of people and places have been changed, my purpose has been to avoid offending those who might have different recollections than I record.

But there is more help that needs acknowledgment. When we did not have enough cash for the down payment on the farm, my brother Lloyd loaned us the extra. Then he sent his son, Brett, to help us get the farm ready for our first summer planting. Some of the children of Laura Johnson, Gayle's sister, came from Idaho during several school vacations to help us. My son Andrew donated his pickup truck to the farm when ours died, and Howard Tucker, Gayle's father, who had already devoted many hours to picking apples and weeding our raspberries, gave us substantial help toward getting other reliable transportation. Clovis and

Nina Romero have been the best of next-farm neighbors from the day we moved in, and Clovis's sharing of his experiences from thirty years as an acequia commissioner has broadened my appreciation for the customs and traditions of our acequia. My understanding of growing apples and other aspects of small farming has been deepened by the books given and loaned by family and friends and acquaintances, including my daughter Susan, my sister Judith, Army Armstrong, Bob Utter, Lucy Cornwell, and others whose names I have forgotten but not their good intentions. The advice and hands-on help of Peter Keegan, Marni's husband and our computer guru, smoothed innumerable bumps in my writing and editing path. Andrea Scharf swapped her house on the Oregon coast for ours, which gave me three critical farm-free weeks to concentrate on finishing the book. Mike and Yvonne Avialotis and family were farm caretakers while we were in Oregon and have given needed help at other times. Celeste Miller and Sarita Pene loaned me their hideaway in Colorado to complete final revisions of the manuscript.

Encouragement and advice have come from many, including Monte and Julia Jordan, John Muste, my sister Marilyn, Beth Hadas of the University of New Mexico Press, and, especially, Charles Cockelreas, who also published "The Study of Ice" and some other parts of the manuscript in *Man, Alive!* the newsletter of the New Mexico Men's Wellness Conference. (A portion of "The Study of Ice" was later reprinted in *The Spirit that Wants Me,* a New Mexico anthology edited by Dianne Duff, Jill Kiefer, and Michelle Miller and published by Duff, Inc., of Albuquerque in 1991.)

As my first reader, Gayle spent many hours going over the manuscript in its various incarnations and provided valuable suggestions for additions, deletions, and revisions. Connie Fulwyler did yeoman service in copyediting and preparing the text for submission. And I owe an immeasurable debt to Dawn Marano of the University of Utah Press for the sensitive reading and the meticulous and creative editing that have helped realize whatever literary virtues this book may have.

Finally, I know this book is not the whole truth of the farm. It says little about interactions with my companion and most important person, how they have shaped my thinking and everything I do. Gayle has read and continues to read more and in more fields than any other person I know, and I am continually stimulated by our conversations and through reading in her substantial library. I owe much to Gayle's wisdom and common sense. To my tendency to fantasize she has brought reality and honesty. That I could get even this far with the truth is a tribute to her persistence.

Cidermaster of Rio Oscuro

Cidermaster of Rio Oscuro

Prologue

WE CAME to farm living with the faith of the innocent. Gayle saw ancient fruit trees, vines growing over fences, mesas and mountains, and the river; it was a spot of beauty on the earth. I saw apple trees, more than I could count, and I wanted to make cider. Inside the old farmhouse the mud walls were thick with grease and grime, the planked ceilings were laced with cobwebs, and the lights were bare bulbs in pull-chain sockets hanging from fraying lamp cords that ran from room to room. The faucets spit and bubbled, and a bucket of water stood beside the toilet to help it flush. The whole farm was a midden of the broken, the used up, the forgotten, and the obsolete.

We had looked at other places. One property topped a promontory between the convergence of the Rio Guadalupe and the Rio Jemez, a few miles up the canyon from Jemez Pueblo. The view was mountains, canyons, red cliffs, and forests, with the rivers on either side below, what ancient hunters, the Anasazi, might have seen long before Columbus and Coronado. One could live in such a place, we thought. There was a small problem: you had to ford the Rio Jemez to get to the house. When we saw it first in April the stream was just a trickle. Anyone could cross it on stepping-stones without getting wet. Then we came back for a second look in May. The trickling Rio Jemez was gone. Snowmelt from the mountains was now raging through the streambed. We asked the owner if a bridge was possible. He had lived there for many years, built the house, planted the fruit trees and grapevines, cultivated the garden. He gave us a crooked smile; a bridge was possible, he said, but he preferred to wait for his crossings until the river allowed them.

We looked at another orchard; it had no clear title. A two-story log house, right on the Rio Grande, had no plumbing. And then we found three acres with three ponds, an unheard-of bounty in New Mexico, and a stunning view of those orange-red cliffs of Jemez Canyon that shone like a second sunrise in the late afternoon, but no shelter we could move into and a building site that was almost inaccessible.

In the process of buying the farm we discovered we had never talked about what each of us wanted. For Gayle the farm meant having animals—geese, ducks, chickens, goats, sheep, and horses. For me it meant growing fruit and protecting trees from animals that ate their fruit. The visual was most important for Gayle. She was a painter. She wanted beautiful surroundings. She did not want an unmowed, run-down look. And if chemicals would help remove the weeds and make vegetables and flowers more appealing, that was all right. To me chemicals, herbicides, pesticides, and chemical fertilizers were anathema, beyond discussion. We also had different tastes in apples. Gayle liked the sweet Delicious, red and yellow; tart apples hurt her tongue. I preferred McIntosh, Jonathan, and Winesap, the apples that made tart cider.

It was our good fortune that the orchard had abundant sweet apples and many varieties of tart. And we did find other ways to remove weeds and improve the soil. And over the years I have learned, if ever so slowly and inconsistently, to discuss with Gayle any plans for chopping, pruning, and cutting. As for the animals, they have become more important to me than I ever imagined they would.

BUYING THE farm took all our money. And so we did what settlers everywhere have done: we began the cleaning, the repair, the rebuilding with our own hands and tools and skills. Then these hands multiplied with the hands and skills of our visiting sons and daughters, of our brothers and sisters, our friends and neighbors and their sons and daughters, and at least once with the hands and special skills and tools of a passing stranger.

We arrived on September sixth. We found the orchard surfeited with apples, pears, and peaches; we found artifacts from farm and home strewn across the ground regardless of their worth or lack of it; and we found unlivable living quarters that for years had been barely maintained by an ailing woman in her nineties, Victoria, and Corina, her diminutive companion-cum-housekeeper in her seventies. Everything cried for immediate attention: unload our belongings, pick the fruit and get it to market, take the junk to the dump and get the valuables under cover, and purge the old house. The whole inside of the old house needed cleaning and repainting and reworking of plumbing and electrical wiring. And we had just two months to get it ready to receive a thousand visitors during the Rio Oscuro studio tour.

I THINK of the apples already ripening on the trees in those early days of our owning the farm and how much we had to learn about picking and pressing, about blending the varieties of apples in much the same way that Gayle and I were learning to blend our families and our lives. From the beginning there was never a question, it seemed, about help arriving when we needed it most. Gayle's brother Tom Tucker and his son Thomas came down from Los Alamos to help unload the rental truck and the two trailers. The next day Anthony Baca from next door came over to help me finish unloading. His wife, Holly Haas, an artist friend of Gayle's, came to help repaint the kitchen. Gayle attacked the crumbling walls of the chapel on her knees. With a small shovel, a trowel, and wheelbarrows of dirt mixed with gypsum, she started to rebuild the walls by hand from the floor up. She patched the walls of the studio with the same mixture. Then we repainted, carefully, to keep the mud plaster from coming off on the roller or the brush. But we needed professional help with the electricity.

Gayle saw a truck on the village road with a sign that read "electrical contractor." She drove after the truck and stopped it. "Do you know anyone who could help rewire our house?" she asked. The man was from Albuquerque. He was working on a contract at the Rio Oscuro elementary school, but he said he would stop by after work. He gave us a shopping list: entrance wire and circuit wire, circuit breakers, a breaker cabinet, boxes, outlets, and switches, and *Wiring Simplified*, a handbook that would help us understand what we were doing.

In a few days he came back. He pulled heavy wire through conduit outside the house, through the eighteen-inch crawl space, and through the ceiling and into the room with the hot water heater where he had put the new breaker cabinet. "I'll come back in a couple of weeks," he said, "to see how you're doing with the wiring."

Son Mark, an architect and sometime custom home builder, came down from Denver. For a week he and Gayle and I chopped and channeled in the dirt and rock walls to put in electrical outlets and switches. Mark stooped and wriggled under the roof to lay circuit wires and to find the holes we had drilled up through dirt and latillas from the bathroom, the hall, the bedroom, the middle room, the studio, and what had been the chapel but would now be Gayle's gallery. And from viga to viga down the length of the blue chapel ceiling Mark put up the electrical track to spotlight her paintings.

While we were working on the house, we were also trying to pick fruit. I put up a U-pick sign on the highway. I called old friends Rex and Jill in Albuquerque. "Do you need any fruit?"

They picked bushels of apples and discovered, on an overgrown drive, six pear trees we didn't know existed. What they picked was what I took for my first trip to the farmers' market in Santa Fe.

The electrical journeyman came back, as he had said he would. We had wired and installed wall outlets and ceiling fixtures in the studio, the gallery, the middle room, and the hall. The rest was roughed in. "This is hard to believe," he said.

"Why?" we asked.

"You're ready to be hooked up. I thought it would take you till spring."

"We had some help."

"And you know how to work."

I did not understand then the importance of those simple words—having help and knowing how to work—to our lives and all we might undertake on this small farm.

When the man finished hooking up the circuits, Gayle asked how much we owed him. He shook his head. No, no, she said; we wanted to pay him. It was all right, he said. Then would he maybe like a painting? Would he come back for the art tour and pick one out? He said he would ask his wife, and he left. He did come back to the tour with his wife, to show her Gayle's work and the house. But he refused to take anything. We have never seen him again, and I cannot remember his name.

Now, fifteen years later, the results of our labors and the generosity of our helpers are everywhere evident. The old stone farmhouse, despite its age and infirmities, is a studio, gallery, and dwelling that many visit and enjoy with us. We have cleared most of the outbuildings. Some, like this writing shed and the cider shed, we have turned to new uses; others have housed our geese and ducks, chickens and peacocks, horses and goats, tractor and tiller, as they housed the animals and machines of our fore-farmers. The broken refrigerator, the broken furniture, and the broken bottles we have recycled or taken to the landfill. The same for the old farming chemicals. And we are now a state-certified organic grower. Hundreds of jars of preserves still in the root cellar when we came were claimed by Corina, last survivor of the old household, and were taken away with the help of her relatives. Hundreds more were left behind along with many bottles of farm-made wine; all had turned bad, and we emptied them. Now the cellar holds what Gayle has put up from our harvests, and some bottles of wine she has made. And there seems no end to our fixing, growing, picking, taking to market, and putting things by. And no end to changes.

BEFORE COMING to the farm I worked fourteen years for engineering and scientific laboratories funded by the United States government. The underlying mission of these laboratories, and all their employees regardless of job titles, was to design, develop, and test nuclear bombs and warheads. We were part of a national defense/deterrence strategy that at its height commanded an unlimited supply of taxpayer dollars and involved one out of every three scientists in the country, one out of five manufacturing workers, and countless numbers of talented people from the social sciences, the humanities, and the arts.

When I met Gayle, she was supporting two sons still in high school, working at the lab part-time doing technical illustrations and art for presentations, teaching art part-time, and painting for herself whenever she could. She was an accomplished watercolor painter and wanted eventually to pursue that full-time. I had been a reporter and taught college English. I ended up editing technical reports at 50 percent more money than the college offered for teaching technical writing and the fine points of composition and analysis of the short story. But what I witnessed and learned in those editing years, and later, about the destruction that has been wrought in the name of national defense, in the name of fear—and the part I played in it all—walks with me in the orchard to this day.

In our two families Gayle and I had seven children. When we bought the farm Connie, her oldest, was creating sculptures of mythical animals out of knotted woolen yarn. She went into art history and specialized in Andean textiles. Rick came to the farm as the original apprentice cidermaster, then went on to college and graduated with majors in anthropology and psychology. James was in the Navy before majoring in biology. Jessica is his daughter.

Mark, my oldest, was an architect in Denver. He and Jacque had one son, Corin, who later renamed himself Peter. Andrew was working in California and came back to New Mexico to manage a laser research laboratory. Susan, my youngest, majored in philosophy and then went into pediatric psychology, which she now teaches at a midwestern university.

Marni, four years older than Susan, graduated cum laude in psychology. She then taught young children dancing and French in private schools in New Mexico and skiing in Colorado. From Colorado she went to Tortola in the British Virgin Islands to crew on a charter sailing boat. She sent picture postcards of the blue, blue waters of the Caribbean. Eventually Marni returned to New Mexico to begin graduate school. Here she met Peter, the love of her life, and gave birth to our grandson Trevor. And here in the place where she grew up she died of cancer.

Children move away, helpers and friends move away. Some come back, again and again. Some never come back. I remember helpers and friends and family when I am pruning grapes, picking pears and apples, making cider, and sometimes sitting at the kitchen table with tea or wine and looking up the hill Gayle and I so often climbed with them. The hill changes with the seasons: new snow, melting snow, rain, green shoots on the chamisa, white blossoms on the Fendler's bush, ripening wild wheat and cheat grass that sticks to my socks, then golden chamisa, cold wind, and snow again.

The geese honk, the dogs bark. I go out, go down the hill. It's nothing; the big gander chases his competitor around the pen, and the other geese and ducks scramble out of the way. I go into the cider shed to check on the apples we are storing in the cooler: Jonathan, Winesap, Red Delicious, Red Rome. I select a Winesap, take out my Swiss Army knife, cut the apple in half. Nineteen years this knife has been in my pocket, ever since Marni brought it back from her year in Switzerland. The lettering is worn off the red casing. A corner of the casing has broken off; I don't know when that happened. I pull out the big blade, cut the apple, bite into it. Juicy, sweet with a backing of tartness. My daughter Marni savored our tart apples, and our old-fashioned Concord and Carmine grapes. Marni of the long dark hair, dancer, French speaker, wife of Peter and mother of Trevor, Marni, who helped us make the very first cider, who banished the tent caterpillars from the orchard, has been gone now six cycles of seasons.

EVERYTHING I have heard from neighbors and outlanders alike, everything I have read, and everything Gayle and I have experienced here has convinced me that it is difficult and sometimes nearly impossible for even the most dedicated people to earn a modest living on a small farm. And this is anywhere, not just in the high, narrow valleys of northern New Mexico, and has been the case with few exceptions for as long as anybody knows. Yet brave, intelligent people, people with many choices, have continued to live on and work small farms, often taking outside jobs to support their farms. On the wall behind me is a poem in Chinese by T'ao Ch'ien, born in 365 C.E., who gave up his position as minister to his emperor to hoe beans in heat and rain. Beata Grant, daughter of neighbors Bob and Carolyn and professor of Chinese literature, has translated it for me.

> Planting beans at the foot of South Mountain:
> Where the grass is thick, the bean sprouts sparse.
> At dawn I try to bring a desultory order to the wild weeds;
> Then, carrying the moon and shouldering my hoe, go home.
> The road is narrow, not only overgrown with grass but long;
> And at the close of day, the dew soaks my clothes through.
> Dew-soaked clothes, however, are scarcely worth complaint:
> As long as they don't mean abandoning the road I've chosen.

One thousand six hundred years later in another country on another continent I read these words and I know T'ao Ch'ien. We walk the same road. It does not matter that he served an emperor before going back to the land and I served an agency of national security. It does not matter that I am pruning trees while he hoed beans. It does not matter that his land was wet and ours is dry and is irrigated through community ditch systems we call acequias. As keepers and caretakers of our farms, our land, and as growers of food for own families and families living in cities where they may not have any land for gardening, he performed and I am performing beneficial work, as beneficial as anything a man or woman can perform.

AFTER WE started making cider I thought of calling this work *A Cidermaster's Handbook*, notes and instructions on keeping an orchard and pressing cider in northern New Mexico. I saw the cidermaster as an equivalent to a Tasmanian cropmaster.

The cropmaster, according to permaculturist Bill Mollison, was the key to the survival of Tasmanian aborigines. He was a man of "long and accurate memory." He was the protector of the tribal tree, the one who set up taboos and feasts and the very manner of taking food. He "ensured that the tribal permaculture endured, even though some of the tribe itself perished."

Like a cropmaster, a cidermaster also needs a long and accurate memory. As keeper of the orchard, he too enforces the taboos. He arranges the manner of preserving the trees and the manner of taking from them. He encourages the orchard spirits and the human spirit in the orchard. He heals the wounds. And as he learns from the living and growing and dying of the trees, he passes on to his helpers all he knows, that the same pure, tart cider he presses now with apples from these trees may still be pressed and enjoyed long after he is gone.

I am still looking for such a cidermaster. Perhaps she or he has not yet incarnated. Until that happens, I record the events of the farm so that when the cidermaster arrives he or she may read what we have done up to this point, and why we did it, and may understand how we felt about being in this work. Perhaps this cidermaster will be an alchemist, transforming people into their essential juices rather than apples into apple juice. After pressing the ten-thousandth gallon of juice, anything seems possible. But with or without the cidermaster, there is no end in sight to the work on the farm. And the inner work, for me, has hardly begun. Blessings are of little value if I do not recognize them and respond to them, to Gayle, to our children and grandchildren, brothers, sisters, friends, neighbors. I am renegotiating the contract with myself to be aware of the blessings I am given by my people, and, yes, our animals, our trees, our land, our acequia, every day, every day.

SOME DAYS this book wanted to organize itself around the cycles of the farm—the blossoms, the fruiting, the harvest, the pressing—and the strangers and friends who have helped us attend them. Some days the only story the book wanted to tell was Marni's story. And some days this book has wanted to organize itself around what Thomas Moore calls the four languages.

Through soul language I hear feelings, I hear the person closest to me, I learn how to speak to her, and live with her. Soul language lets me hear trees, rocks, dirt, and gives meaning to murmurings in the chicken pen.

Spirit language lets me hear the moon, the planets, and the great constellations as I listen on an evening walk to the crickets, the river, and my own flowing blood. Spirit language gives me access to the *akashic* record, to all that has been said and done since the creation of the universe.

Mind language gives me access to the records, the facts, the history as found in documents and anecdotes, and lets me convert them into verse.

And body language gives me access to movement, paying attention to body and gravity, being careful not to fall out of trees anymore.

But the four languages refuse to coexist. Each one competes for my attention, as now, for example, when I try to select a language to talk about the presence of a Cold War artifact in the goose pen.

We use the inverted cover of an old missile container as a watering trough for the Toulouse geese. Inscriptions on its top instruct military personnel on the proper storage and handling temperatures, pressures, tools, procedures, and inventorying. I smile as I read these instructions in the pen of the blustering geese under the great walnut tree. I remember the Second World War and the Cold War. I remember the missiles, which our elected leaders called swords of peace. I might look at this cover as a piece of the peace. My lifting it each morning to empty the thick goose muck and rinse it and refill it with fresh water might be my ritual, my prayer for preserving our rural tranquillity. But some future farmer's son might ask his father about this heavy aluminum cover, and I wonder in what language he might answer.

AND IN what language should I honor the work of my partner, the artist, she who communicates in light and color? Gayle's vision infuses mine in more ways than I know. She breaks down the walls of a lifetime, lets in the sun, and surrounds us with flowers. Her paintings put food on the table in the long season between crops, and when crops are frosted thin. We talk, we talk, we talk. Sometimes I think we might benefit from a fifth language, one that transforms us as we speak.

In the end, perhaps all languages merge. The book defies my attempts at organization as it defied definition. As the farm itself defies my attempts at organization and definition. And so this book about our farming life has become just that, the book of the farm, what we who came as innocents have learned, about our farm and about ourselves, as we have lived here.

BOOK 1

The Study of Ice

PART 1

The First Cider

When we press the pomace
and the juice flows
again and again,
we come to believe in forever.
THE CIDERMASTER'S HANDBOOK

ABOUT A MONTH after we moved onto the land, sometime in October it was, Marni brought a friend from her dance class at the University of New Mexico to see the farm, to help pick apples, and to make the first cider. Marni and Charles took a couple of boxes down into the orchard, and I got on the phone.

Someone had told us that Carl Berghofer, whose orchard and fruit stand were on the Taos highway, had a small cider press that he didn't mind loaning within the community. We tracked it to another neighbor who was happy to drop it off, if he could use it himself later.

The little press arrived just as Marni and Charles were coming up the drive, each carrying a box of fresh-picked apples. We set the press on a table on the wooden bridge over the arroyo. On top of the frame we read the inscription: Acme Lard Press. Neither Marni nor Charles nor Gayle nor I had ever actually made cider, and this inscription did not give us a lot of confidence.

Inside the steel frame was a perforated steel basket. Over the basket was a screw-type gear. At the bottom of the basket was a round piece of wood. We decided that once the apples were inside we should place the wooden cover on top of them and then screw it down and down until the juice came out.

We took a dishpan full of apples from the boxes Marni and Charles had picked, washed them, and then the four of us, each with a paring knife, stood there in the sun on that bright October afternoon cutting up apples until we filled the steel basket. Now we set the cover on top and started turning the handle. I turned, Gayle turned, Marni turned, Charles turned. We mashed the pieces of apple into the bottom of the basket, but no juice ran into the bowl.

"Something is wrong," I said.

"Yes, Dad," Marni said, and we all laughed.

"Maybe we have to grind the apples first," Gayle said.

Of course!

We fed the fruit into a hand-cranked meat grinder, then poured the ground apples back into the pressing basket. Now the old lard press cum cider press came through; thick, golden, chunky juice bubbled out of the basket into a big pot. I ladled it into our glasses.

Marni raised her glass. "To your new farm, Dad and Gayle."

"And to the first cider," I added, "and to health."

We drank. A little chunky, because we had not thought to strain the juice, yet through the chunks was the sweet-tart flavor of fresh apples.

"I like this," Marni said. And we all smiled.

After Marni and Charles went back to Albuquerque with some apples and a little jar of cider, Gayle and I considered the project. The efforts of four people washing and cutting and grinding and turning the crank had yielded only a gallon of cider, however good it tasted. As soon as we had the time we had to find a real cider press.

The next year Bob and Carolyn Grant, whose farm was the first one up the road in the village of Rio Oscuro, invited us to try the combination chopper and press that Bob had made from plans in the organic farming magazine. Bob was a writer as well as a small farmer. He had published two novels and many short stories. I remembered having read his story on growing apples in New Mexico; it won the O. Henry Award for best American short story in 1957. I was in graduate school in Iowa City when I read "My Apples," and, though I'd never been to the Southwest and had never grown apples and had read and forgotten hundreds of stories about familiar experiences, something about Bob's story stuck in my memory. Perhaps it was the ending. The young couple had rented a small house in an orchard in New Mexico and the farmer promised them the apples from the biggest tree, which was right next to their house. All summer they watched their apples grow and ripen. And then came the day of harvest. The farmer's wife and her son picked all the trees in the orchard and loaded them on a big truck with a Texas license plate. Then they started picking the tree next to the little house. The young man tried to stop them; the farmer had promised these apples to him and his wife when they rented the house. The woman cursed him. Her son told him to get out of the way. The young man looked for the farmer; he was nowhere. The couple decided to move as soon as possible. The next day the farmer came over to apologize, to explain his wife's problems; next year for sure, he said, they could have the apples. So they stayed. And the next year all the blossoms froze.

On the way over to see his cider machine, I asked Bob if his story was about a true experience. He laughed. "I couldn't make up anything like that."

"And did the frost actually get all the fruit the next year?"

"You can ask Carolyn, or you can wait and see for yourself what can happen to your fruit."

Bob's machine was nothing like the old lard press we had borrowed the first year from Carl Berghofer. Bob's was made of wood. It had two compartments. In the first was a wooden drum studded with nails. Bob threw some apples into the compartment and began turning the handle. As the drum rotated the nails cut the apples into a coarse mash or pomace. Now he pushed the first batch of pomace into the next compartment. Under this compartment was an old mechanical automobile jack. After several rounds of grinding apples into pomace, the compartment was full. Then Bob began pumping the jack, which, inch by inch, forced the pomace against the wooden top. The juice started flowing. Bob kept pumping until he got about a gallon of juice from the pomace. Now he smiled. "Not bad, huh?"

No, not bad at all, I said. We emptied the used pomace into his wheelbarrow, and then I tried his machine. Put in the apples, turn the handle till they were ground, push pomace into the pressing compartment till it was full, then jack it up. Not much cider came out, but the machine worked. Could I borrow it?

"Of course," he said, and we lifted the machine onto the bed of his old pickup and drove over to our farm. This felt good. This was a beginning.

As we slid Bob's machine out of the truck, one of its legs came loose. "No problem," I said, and I sent Bob home with many thanks. Next morning I screwed the leg back on and set up his homemade cider machine under the wide eaves of the big shed. I got my apples and started to chop. A nail fell out of the roller and into the mash. I fished it out. Then two more nails fell out. I hammered them back in. Next day more came out. I was running out of places to drive them in. I felt foolish. I had thought we could get into real cider making with this homemade wooden press. Then the crank handle broke. And finally the boards holding the jack came loose and the jack fell off.

I called Bob and apologized for breaking his press. He said not to worry, it had broken before. "How would you like to see a demonstration of a real cider press?" he asked. I asked when. He told me that Fred Martinez and his father, Delfin, who had a big orchard up the river, had just bought a new grinder and a new press. He would find out when they were pressing and ask if we could come over and watch.

The equipment was set up outside, right in the orchard.

Several other neighbors were also on hand for the demonstration. Bob introduced me to Fred and his father. "He's our new neighbor. He wants to make cider."

"Good." We shook hands. "This is the grinder," Fred said. "It has a one-horsepower motor." He flipped the switch. The grinder hummed. Fred's helper lifted a full box of apples and dumped the whole thing into the hopper. Whoosh! In just forty-five seconds he had a bucketful of pomace as fine as applesauce.

Another helper poured the pomace onto a rack on the cider press. Another bushel, another rack. When the press was stacked full, Fred pumped the hydraulic jack. The juice started to flow, and the helpers started filling bottles. "We get twenty gallons of cider per pressing," Fred said, "sometimes as much as twenty-three. That's about three-and-a-half gallons per bushel."

I went home and told Gayle what I had seen. We talked about the cost. I talked with Fred on the phone. He said he had researched all the small cider presses on the market before they bought, and they were pleased. He dropped off the literature and also ads for other presses.

The press and grinder together was too big an investment for us that first year. We talked to Bob. "Why don't you just buy the press?" he said. "Maybe we can borrow a grinder for you to start with."

When the press arrived we set it up on the deck over the arroyo, the same place where we had started with Carl's lard press the year before. The next day Bob took me over to the small winery in Rio Oscuro and introduced me to Mike and Pat Johnson, who owned it and ran it. I was the new neighbor, Bob told them, and I had just bought a press to make cider, but I didn't have a grinder. Mike said he wanted to get out of the cider business and just concentrate on wine making. "He could borrow our grinder, couldn't he, Pat?"

"Sure."

"And you can supply the people I used to sell our cider to in Taos."

We loaded Mike and Pat's grinder onto Bob's pickup, drove it over to the farm, and unloaded it onto the deck next to our new press.

I picked apples in our orchard. Then young Olaf, a neighbor from down the road who used to help make cider at the winery, came over to help us. And so we started again on the bridge over the arroyo, making pomace with Mike and Pat's grinder, loading the racks on the new press, pumping the jack until the juice flowed, taking turns standing in the arroyo to fill the gallon jugs by gravity, and then capping them and lining them up on the picnic table.

OLAF HAD worked on the farm as a teenager before we came, irrigating the orchard, driving the tractor, and picking fruit. He also painted, played the guitar, and took singing lessons. Now in his twenties, fair-haired, medium height, a little on the stocky side, he might have been taken for someone who had wrestled in high school if it were not for the shy, uncertain, quizzical look he might wear when asked a question, or asked to do something. He had been in the state mental hospital in Las Vegas for treatment of schizophrenia and was released on the condition that he take medication. Sometimes he took his medication, and sometimes he didn't. But I found him willing, friendly, and usually pleasant to have around.

One day I took Olaf with me to pick an orchard in Cañoncito, a few miles up the road from Rio Oscuro. At the time he was taking voice lessons in Santa Fe. He climbed into the first tree and started to sing. The higher into the trees he climbed, the louder he sang. When he had filled his picking bag, he climbed down, emptied the apples into a box, carried the ladder to another tree, and climbed up. Then the singing began again.

Olaf sang while he picked apples, while he ground the apples into pomace, while he filled the jugs with fresh cider. He sang, and sometimes the cider overflowed into the arroyo. Sometimes he threw apples into the grinder without replacing the barrel, and the pomace sprayed over the deck. Sometimes he just stood on the ladder singing to the tree, the apples, and the sky. But Olaf was good-natured, and a tap on the shoulder would bring him back.

The last day of that first real season of cider making Olaf took home a couple of gallons of cider for his parents and his fellow students in the singing class. He was going to stay in Santa Fe that night; his father had given him money for a motel room. But he did not come home the next day. On the morning of the second day he knocked on our door. No, he had not been home yet; he was just getting back from Santa Fe. We asked him to sit down and have breakfast with us. He did. He had his music with him, and Gayle asked which songs he was working on. Gayle knew one of them and they sang it together, and Olaf seemed to be happy with himself. But once he got home after being gone the two nights he told his parents he didn't want to see himself anymore, and he started breaking mirrors, and he broke every mirror in the house. Finally his father took him back to the hospital.

Over the years, when he was around and when he was able, Olaf helped us with many projects. We cut deadwood in the orchard. He worked the cement mixer when we poured the walkway along the acequia. We hauled firewood in his father's old pickup. He began the mud plastering of this writing house. Together he and I lifted the roof off the old goose pen, set four new posts, and put the roof on top of them to make a shed to store apple boxes.

One day he helped Gayle whitewash the front of the house under the portal. "The wind is blowing," he said. "The wind is sad today."

Olaf always smiled when we worked together, and many times it was hard to believe anything was wrong with him. I asked once when we were down in the orchard cutting out deadwood what he would like to do with his life.

He thought for a moment. "I guess I want to have my horse again."

"What kind of horse did you have?"

"It wasn't exactly mine," he said, smiling. "I found it in the arroyo. It was hungry. We fed it. I took care of it, for a long time."

"What happened to it?"

"My father kept looking for the owner. And one day he found him, and the man took the horse."

"Did you ever see the horse again?"

"I don't know," Olaf said. He thought for a moment. "I can't remember. But I would like to have that horse again."

We loaded the wood in the trailer and moved to another tree. "You have a lot of talent," I said. "You could do something with painting, and with the guitar."

He looked at me, frowning, as if trying to remember something. "I am not the person I used to be," he said. "I have lost a lot of myself. It's gone, just gone."

"The medication?"

"Yes. That's it."

After that we didn't see Olaf for a year. We heard he was back in the hospital. We heard that he was so unhappy he jumped out of a window, landed on a roof. A new doctor changed his medication. He got better. He was able to move to a halfway house in Santa Fe. Then one morning three years later he came up our road on his bicycle. I was out in the orchard, irrigating. He didn't see me.

"Olaf!" I called.

He stopped, put down the bike, came over to the fence. He smiled. We shook hands.

"You're looking good."

He gazed at me, seemed about to speak, but no words came.

"I'm glad to see you! Glad you came over."

He nodded. He looked over the orchard, the water now running down rows beyond the pump house. I thought of the days he had spent here with me. I thought of the years before we came, his seasons working for Victoria, climbing their old wooden picking ladders, then carrying the boxes of fruit up for

Corina to sort. When he was fourteen and fifteen and sixteen. With his whole life in front of him. Now he was twenty-six. "We've been thinking about you," I said, "wondering how you were doing."

He turned from the orchard and looked at me with his shy, quizzical look. "I've been thinking about you, too," he said. "How is Gayle?"

I climbed through the fence. I put my arm around him, gave him a squeeze. I wanted him to know that I cared for him, and that Gayle cared for him, too. I picked up the shovel. "Let's go see how she is." He picked up his bike, and we walked up the hill.

I HAVE no record of how much cider Olaf and I made that October we worked together. I do know that Kay Weiner, another neighbor, brought us two hundred gallon bottles from Albuquerque in the back of her small car. I know that we pressed seventy-five gallons on the last day of the season and sold them all the weekend of the studio tour. And the next year we bought our own grinder, the same model Fred and Delfin had. I touch, I smell, I grope for more details. But now a hundred-hundred other memories fall upon me.

October comes around again, and I stand on the twelve-foot ladder, the picking bag full on my chest. I feel the weight of all the boxes I have filled with apples today, and I am tired. Yet on the branch above me there are still a few large apples, the old-fashioned Romes that make our cider aromatic. I could climb down, empty my bag, and forget it. Or I could get them: balance, reach, lean, stretch, pick. I stretch toward those perfumed Romes, and the tips of my fingers barely touch the nearest one. What is the sense of this? I smile. The effort has no logic. Another few apples in the box will hardly swell the flow of juice from the cider press. And who will care whether these are picked or not? I do not think the tree cares. And who if not the tree? No one in the orchard watches me.

I climb to the very top of the twelve-foot, three-legged picking ladder, two steps higher than the last safe step, and I reach out. Balanced as if on a wire over the river, balanced as only one who has fallen will balance, now one-footed I grasp the apple and its neighbor and the neighbor's neighbor and bring them back, into the bag. And I flash back to that tree in Leila's orchard up the river, Leila holding her baby on her hip watching us pick, how tired I was but having to pick anyway with my son Andrew to fill a two hundred–bushel order because the two pickers had gotten drunk with what I paid them the day before and said they wouldn't pick that day. I am so tired, standing on the ten-foot ladder, the picking bag on my chest full of apples, that I close my eyes for an instant, and as I start to fall I grab a leg of the picking ladder, and it pulls up and I fall backwards, and the ladder and the full picking bag land on top of me. After seconds, minutes perhaps, I open my eyes, look up into the frowning face of Andrew standing over me and Leila bending down to bandage my bleeding head with a diaper. Andrew starts to help me sit up, and the movement makes me feel sick, and my head spins. "No, no," I say, and he lets me down again. He calls Gayle and she rushes over, and then they wait with me, and finally my head quiets enough so I can get into the car and Gayle can drive me down to the clinic. And for six months afterwards I see double every time I sit up.

I climb down so carefully now I lose not a single fruit from the overflowing bag. I untie the flap. The apples unload themselves into the box. I am too tired to be pleased. Still, I work at it. I breathe in and calm the body, breathe out and smile.

WE FIRST saw the farm in June 1983. In September, with all our goods in the rented truck and trailers and our van, with hope and expectations, with open hands and empty pockets we rolled up the road into Obscurana's bosom overflowing with ripe and ripening apples, pears, peaches, plums, and grapes. We embraced the new fruit and the old orchards and vineyards and the over-grown irrigation laterals with their crumbling gates, and the pens for chickens, ducks, geese, and peacocks, and the great pole barn filled with empty fruit boxes and all the other large and small farm buildings. We took possession of the old homestead perched between the acequia and the hill amidst heaps of leavings on the porches and in the drive, the rotting decks and bridges, the mud-and-stone house with its ready-to-leak tin roof, its bare bulbs strung on fraying fabric cords, its sputtering faucets, and its slow-draining toilet. Everything here was ours, and everything called at one and the same time for our attention. We had bought the farm.

And with the farm came all of the present and the past, the human history of all the people who had lived and labored and died here from the beginning of time, recorded or not. And the history of all that grew here and was planted here, from apples to roses, prickly pear to sage. And the geology of this earth itself. Today, after many years, I reopen the "Abstract of Title" to this farm to see what if any of this history it contains. The first document is a copy of the patent from the General Land Office of the United States of America.

WHEREAS there has been deposited in the General Land Office of the United States a certificate numbered 483 of the Register and Receiver at Santa Fe, New Mexico, whereby it appears that, under the provisions of the Act of Congress approved March 3, 1891, entitled "an Act to establish a court of private land claims. . ." the claim of Luciano Trujillo, Grantee of Severo Trujillo has been duly established to the following described land. . . .

NOW KNOW YE that the United States of America, in consideration of the premises, and in conformity with the provisions of the acts aforesaid has given and granted and by these presents does give and grant unto said Luciano Trujillo the tract of land above described TO HAVE AND TO HOLD the said tracts . . . and to his heirs and assigns forever. . . .

Given under my hand, at the City of Washington, the

second day of April in the year of our Lord one thousand nine hundred and eight and of the Independence of the United States one hundred and thirty-second.

By the President

Theodore Roosevelt
By M. W. Young, Secretary
H. W. Sanford,
Recorder of the General Land Office.

With such words the possession of private holdings in the New World is upheld and protected for the people of record, the grantees of Severo Trujillo and his brethren. With the same sort of words the heirs of the people of no record are everywhere excluded "forever." No matter that the Picuris hunted here and farmed here and danced here to their sacred spirits for a thousand years before Europeans "discovered" this "New World." If the Spanish crown, or the Republic of Mexico, or the United States General Land Office did not recognize this use, then it had no standing.

In that October four hundred years ago when the Spanish army invaded the valley of Rio Oscuro, the Picuris—men, women, and children—abandoned their lands and villages and fled to the mountains. The army burned the villages, burned crops, destroyed the houses. Then it snowed in the mountains and many Picuris died. The survivors took refuge with the Apaches. Eventually, a few returned.

It was Picuris warriors who organized and led the pueblo revolt against the Spanish in 1680. Before the Spanish, the Picuris inhabited land from the high mountains to the Rio Grande. At their peak they numbered six thousand, the largest pueblo tribe in what is now New Mexico. Legends speak of buildings in the village ten stories high. Today official Picuris lands are but a shadow of what they were. And on this farm there is no trace of the Picuris. Or so we thought, until just last year.

The next document in the abstract, dated March 22, 1935, is a warranty deed to Victoria Howser and Annelise Schaffle from

Luciano Trujillo and Anna Trujillo, his wife. Immediately following that is a warranty deed from Howser and Schaffle to Friedrich Meyers for the sum of one dollar. Another warranty deed dated twenty-one years later conveyed the property from the Reverend Friedrich Meyers to Victoria Howser "for consideration paid." The final document is the power of attorney Victoria Howser gave to Thomas McKinnon on March 5, 1982. She was then ninety-two.

FRIEDRICH MEYERS had been dead twenty-six years when we took over the farm. Annelise Schaffle had followed him in 1966. Victoria had just died, in March, at ninety-three. Corina Coronada, in her seventies, was the only survivor of the household.

We came with a realtor from Santa Fe. Corina opened the door just enough to see who we were. Bruce, the realtor, introduced us. I put out my hand, and she touched it with her small hand, like bird pecking at grain. She was tiny, under five feet. Bruce was over six feet. He tried to bend, to hunch up, as if to appear less overpowering. Corina looked up at him. She did not have to sell, she began. Thomas McKinnon, Victoria's lawyer, had told her that. Father Meyers had given Victoria the farm before he died, and now Victoria had left it to her. It was true that Victoria's relatives from California, the nieces and nephews who used to come here to play as children, wanted their money; but she was living here. She had her rights.

She paused. Bruce said nothing. She went on. But how was she going to take care of everything, all of it, by herself? A tiny woman like her? No, the lawyer had not asked her that part, but she knew what he was thinking.

And she could still see him, for all that white hair, as the little Thomas whom she had taken care of those summers his family sent him to the farm, to help Father with the weeding and irrigating and whatever else he could do. She had taken good care of this Thomas McKinnon, and now she did listen to him. And she trusted him as much as anyone, for what else can a poor woman do? After she had given her whole life to this place, and these people. Where was Victoria now? Where was Father? Why was it up to her to make such a decision, to sell the farm?

As we stood there on the porch, under the bare tin roof, the three of us, next to the broken basket chairs, the old refrigerator with its door open, the blackened strings of chile and perhaps jerky hanging from rusty nails in the beam and on the posts, Corina presented us with bits and pieces of what had happened decades earlier. They were like entries from a diary she had been keeping for fifty years, entries seemingly selected and read at random. Finally, she stopped and opened the door. And she took us down the five steps to the lower level where Friedrich Meyers had lived and died.

Victoria and Corina had kept Father Meyers's study and sleeping space and the chapel next door like a museum. Just outside the doorway hung his white shirts, his trousers, his jackets, his pastorly vestments. Inside, the pastor's desk stood against the front wall, under a bare lightbulb dangling from a frayed, fabric-covered electric cord. Behind the desk were three deep-set wooden casement windows, one with hinges and two still nailed in place as on the day they were set. Between the desk and the outside door were two straight chairs and an upholstered chair.

Four stacks of bookshelves separated the study and the sleeping area. I saw books on history and politics, on religion and philosophy. There was an old German nature book with pictures of the flowers and trees that grew in the homeland. All seemed to be exactly as Friedrich Meyers had left it twenty-six years earlier. In the corner, next to the gas heater, was a single bed. And on the wall above the bed was his motto embroidered in red: *Erwachet froh jeder Morgen*, Wake up joyful every morning.

I wonder what Corina understood by this motto. Would it have been a day of joy if her mentor awakened? And how would she have wanted to see him? As on the day he sanctified the chapel, in vestments of white and gold, saying mass here for the first time? Or as the robust farmer-priest in the photograph Corina showed us, a framed black-and-white of household Obscurana, which hung on one wall of the study? Father Meyers and

Victoria stood in the middle, big people, tall people, looking straight ahead. Annelise was on the right, smaller, smiling, and Corina on the left, smallest of all, a kerchief over her head, holding a big fish. Meyers looked maybe forty-five, Victoria a little younger, and Corina probably in her late twenties. I thought the picture should have a title: Obscurana, the day we caught the big fish.

OUTSIDE FATHER Meyers's studio, just beyond his chapel, Corina showed us an old apple tree whose boughs stretched across the acequia, a tree so ideal in shape that it would stir cherished memories in anyone who had climbed trees as a child. It was June, and the apples hanging from branches, some just a few feet above the water, were still small and green. But this tree grew "very big, red apples" Corina said, and she extended her thin arm with her small palm open to show us how big. Her uncle had made this tree. He brought a cutting from his orchard and grafted it to the crab apple already growing here. It was a gift for Father Meyers. As she stood there beneath the tree, talking and looking up into the apples and the foliage, I knew that this old forked trunk and all its great bent limbs and branches owed life to this tiny but insistent woman. Corina had watered this tree, while the scion was taking hold, blending its cambium and bark into the nurturing stock, and she continued tending it year by year as the tree outgrew her and outgrew the small crab foster tree and reached up and out over the water. She had adopted the graftling born before her eyes, as she had adopted the chickens she raised, the rabbits, the turkeys, the grapevines she planted, the children of the farm.

Only now do I begin to understand why Corina showed us that tree; she imagined we might carry on her vigil.

And she was right.

I would go down into the orchard and find a small apple tree almost lying on the ground, maybe knocked over by a breathless galloping horse, or dropped by some animal that had chomped away half its root, or some other small calamity. I would find a dead branch with a fork, cut it and trim it, and lift the little tree and prop it up. And the tree would fall over. And I would get rope and stakes and a hammer, pull the tree up straight and tie it firmly in four directions. And at least once a week I would check the ropes, tighten some, loosen others. After three or four years when the roots had renewed themselves I would remove three ropes and leave just one for steadiness, and in the seventh year that, too, I would take off. And when the fruit came, it would be a surprise; perhaps a sweet, rich-flavored dessert apple of a variety I had never tasted and would never be able to name.

My path through the orchard season to season was the road to mecca. Every turn thrust an opportunity for helping or healing a tree with shovel or saw or pruning shears, for digging the extra water ditch, sawing the dead limbs, cutting out the overlapping branches and clearing the sprouts to open the tree's center to the sun. Sometimes I would stray from the path, follow birds and butterflies, wander in the wildflowers, or stop to watch the clouds. Yet the little I have given to our orchard has been returned a hundredfold, every spring in the sea of rippling whites and pinks and in the gold and red flavors of fall.

I learned the name of Corina's very large red apples when I took them to the Santa Fe Farmers' Market the next year: Wolf River. Angelina Valdez, a warm and smiling vendor who brought in polished, perfect fruit from the orchard she and her husband tended in Velarde, had two bushels of Wolf River, none smaller than a giant grapefruit. The apple is an early American variety that originated in Fremont, Wisconsin, and was named for the river nearby. The Wolf River with its red and crimson skin is a handsome apple and the largest in our orchard; I've picked a Wolf River in November that was larger than a baby's head. When fully ripe it is crisp and juicy with a complex flavor; I just begin to appreciate that flavor after the third or fourth bite. Several customers in Santa Fe have called Wolf River the best pie apple and come back for it year after year. And it also blends well into our cider.

Some of the varieties of apples in our orchard originated more than 150 years ago. Maidenblush is one of them. The fruit is large and flat and round with a bright red cheek on a yellow background. Southmeadow Fruit Gardens of Lakeside, Michigan, which specializes in vintage apples, places Maidenblush among the choice old American apples. An orchardist in 1827 described it as "tender and sprightly, remarkably light and fitted for drying."

Both Wolf River and Maidenblush are included in the list of 152 choice dessert apples, "from among the thousands of apple varieties known and named," that have been propagated and were offered by Southmeadow to home fruit gardeners in its 1995 catalog. Although we have more trees now than I can manage, a few of the varieties listed would fit very well in our orchard. Calville Blanc d'Hiver (White Winter Calville), grown as the finest of dessert apples for Louis XIII in seventeenth-century France and included in Thomas Jefferson's collection of best fruit varieties at the beginning of the nineteenth century in Virginia, is one I could find a sunny place for. Robert Nitschke, compiler of the Southmeadow list and chairman of the Fruit Gardens Committee of the American Pomological Society, describes Calville Blanc as having "tender, spicy flesh with a delicate banana-like aroma." It is served for dessert in the finest restaurants of Paris. And in studies of vitamin C in apples, Calville Blanc came out with thirty-five to forty milligrams per one hundred grams of pulp, highest of all apples in the study and almost twice as high as an orange.

Rhode Island Greening would also be welcome, along with Hidden Rose. The Greening has been a favorite cooking apple and dessert apple since colonial times. I have a picture in the cider shed of a Greening during harvest, limbs spread out in all directions and dozens of full boxes underneath. Hidden Rose was "discovered" at a cider mill in Oregon when one Louis Kimsey took a bite of a greenish yellow apple that had fallen out of a box and found solid rose flesh inside along with a rich flavor. Kimsey then traced the fruit to a large, old tree growing on an abandoned farm. Hidden Rose could add both new flavor and color to our cider.

And I wouldn't mind having one of the good old English "cyder" apples, the kind Richard Roney-Dougal, a friend in Rio Oscuro, remembers from his father's farm in Britain. "They were bitter, you know. You wouldn't want to eat them," he said. "But they made great cider." Southmeadow offered five such apples—Dabinett, Foxwhelp, Kingston Black, Medaille d'Or, and Tremlett's Bitter—each with the proper balance of sugar, acid, and tannin to make a vintage cider, not a blend. Any one of them would be fine.

Some of our other apples are probably versions of established commercial varieties upgraded by nurseries to make them more visually appealing to buyers. Our Double Red trees, for example, produce apples with skins that turn almost black even before full ripeness, yet taste to my palate about the same as apples from the Delicious trees in the next row whose skins are of only moderate redness. The orchard has a dozen apple varieties, common and uncommon, that I can name, and perhaps another dozen whose names I do not know or am not sure of. They may all be on Southmeadow's lists, among the favorite dessert apples, or among the twenty-seven commercial orchard varieties, or among their conservation crab apples propagated for people who want to plant trees for birds and other wildlife. A few, however, will not be on their lists. One small yellow apple, which grows along the drive next to the raspberry patch, is so bitter that I will not bite into it anymore, no matter how appealing it looks when all the other apples are picked. But it grows on half of an old tree whose other half has large red and yellow apples in the old-fashioned Rome family, so I indulge the one half for the sake of the other. Another tree with medium-size, bitter red apples is vigorous and growing in a choice location in the main orchard. I indulge this tree because I hope someday to graft onto it something good.

CIDERING IS special in New Mexico. We do not have the great apple orchards and cider tradition of New England and New

York. And the large apple orchards we do have grow mainly Red Delicious, that big-shouldered, pointed, deep-colored fruit that makes a sweet, bland, almost flavorless juice. I remembered liking the taste of McIntosh apples when I was growing up in Connecticut—McIntosh as eating apples, in my mother's pies, and in the cider we would buy at farms in the fall. I wanted to make that kind of cider, a cider that gave you a mouthful of flavor and a little tartness, a cider with a McIntosh-type complex flavor. In our first year I had no idea there were any McIntosh on this farm. Amidst all the Red Delicious I was delighted to find the Jonathans and the Winesaps and large, aromatic apples that turned out to be old-fashioned Romes. It was not till the third year that I discovered we did indeed have some McIntosh, a dozen old trees, and five McIntosh-types that ripen early, at the beginning of August.

When I started going to the Santa Fe Farmers' Market with cider made from Yellow Transparent, Jonathan, McIntosh, and Winesap I had two types of responses. For people raised in the Southwest and Texas it was usually too "tart"; it puckered their lips. But for transplants and visitors from Michigan, New York, and New England, our cider was just right, just like back home, maybe even better.

"Just like back home"—I must have heard that a hundred times over the last ten years, along with the thanks of people who appreciate the way we make cider only from unsprayed, handpicked apples. In truth, the quality of our cider comes from the unique character of our orchard and is independent of our technique or stewardship. Gayle bought me a copy of Annie Proulx's booklet "Making the Best Apple Cider," which further confirmed what we had discovered about Obscurana. Proulx sets forth five classifications of cider apples: high acid, medium acid, low acid, aromatic, and astringent. In our orchard, unlike any other orchard I know of in this valley, all five are represented, including Jonathan, high acid; McIntosh and Winesap, medium acid; Golden Delicious, Red Delicious, and Red Rome, low acid; old-fashioned Rome and McIntosh, aromatic; and crab apple, astringent (which we do not use).

And in the orchard the different varieties ripen at different times during the growing season. We can usually start making tart summer cider around August 15th using our Yellow Transparent and, if they haven't been frosted out, the early McIntosh. In our best years, we run through October and even into November with Winesap, old-fashioned Rome, and Wolf River.

The balance of varieties is only part of the equation. Our Jonathans, for example, seem more flavorful than any others around here. I discovered the difference when picking Jonathans in a neighbor's orchard. They tasted like Jonathans from which all the overtones and undertones had been removed. I tried Jonathans from another orchard along the Rio Grande. The same. I asked that grower, David Vaeth, who had twelve hundred apple trees, whether he believed there could be such a difference in flavor between his Jonathans and ours.

"Of course," he said. "You have the old varieties, before the nurseries bred out flavor and bred in looks. I wish I had trees like yours."

Dave Slagle, a pecan farmer and poet from Las Cruces, suggests that the age of our apple trees may be a factor in the flavor as it is with grapevines; weathered old trees, like old vines, stressed by the years, the good seasons and the bad, produce fruit of richer character and more complex flavors than young trees and young vines. Perhaps.

It's been a half-century and more since Victoria and Friedrich planted this orchard. Even counting the replacements, the average age of our trees may be close to fifty years. Over this time the trees may have created a communal balance in which each relates to the whole and to each other in a mutually beneficial way. Each tree and each part of the orchard may have adapted in its own way to wind pattern, soil, irrigation water, orchard grasses and wildflowers and bees and other insects, ions and gases in the air, humidity, rain and snow, intensity of the sun, and the presence of animals and people. And if these adaptations have been interactive, they would influence each other in a mutual discovery, mutual learning process. How this process might work is the lifetime study of the cidermaster.

Such adaptations and interactions are not implausible if one considers the latest discoveries in plant-science laboratories. Researchers have found that tobacco plants produce a chemical to ward off a plant disease, and they communicate to neighboring plants that the disease is present, and they in turn produce the chemical. If tobacco plants do this, then so may other plants. And sixty-year-old apple trees as well.

BY THE beginning of our third harvest year, it was clear that we would have plenty of apples. We had all the equipment: cider press, new grinder, juice pump, bottles, caps, and labels that read "Big Willow Cider." The name described the most prominent and robust tree on the farm, the weeping willow next to the tractor shed whose diameter was five feet at ground level and swelled to seven or eight feet where its limbs branched out over the drive in one direction and the acequia in the other. Big Willow seemed a happier sound for cider than Obscurana, something dark or hidden.

Gayle's son Richard had been telling us that his job in Pocatello was a dead end. I wondered if he would like to help us out. And this began what I call the four-year family period of cider making. By the end of that time, we had established a place for our blended, slightly tart cider at the Santa Fe Farmers' Market and a half-dozen retail stores in the area. I had learned what farming and cidering required of me in terms of skill and energy. What I did not know was what level of effort Gayle and I could sustain or should sustain over time. And I could not, of course, predict what would happen that was beyond our control, and in the hands of nature.

On our first day working together, Rick and I picked fifteen bushels of tart red apples, mostly Johnnies and Macs. The next day, bright and early, we had a quick breakfast of oatmeal and went down to set up the press under the wide eaves of the same old shed where I had tried out and broken Bob's homemade press the year before. It was ten o'clock when we finally started grinding the first bushel, a sunny morning in the second week in September. We had a beach umbrella over the press as protection from the sun. As we were loading pomace on the racks, clouds appeared, and then just as we began squeezing the juice, a sudden gust of wind blew over the big umbrella. And before we could right it, the rain started. The storm passed as quickly as it had appeared, and the sun came out again, but it was obvious we needed another, less exposed place to work.

Later in the day Rick and I went for a walk. "How about in here?" he said when we reached the tractor shed. We considered the possibilities; there was an electric outlet, plenty of space for equipment and apples, and protection on three sides. And as far as I knew, the roof didn't leak. "Could you move the tractor and these things?" he said, pointing to the disk and the blade.

"Sure. And we could put a tarp over the front."

I started the tractor, and in short order we had the shed cleared. In the morning we would rake out our new workplace, smooth the dirt, lay down plywood, and set up the press and the grinder. I felt good. Things seemed to be working out now that Rick was here.

That night it started to rain, a light drizzle. Then the rain cloud moved over the mesa above our farm, hung there, and let loose. After fifteen minutes the arroyo started to run. The bubbling brown flood of liquid silt ran over the acequia, over the boards that were supposed to hold it in its channel, over the road, and on down the hill.

It was morning before the rain stopped and we could look over the damage. In the tractor shed, on top of what was supposed to be the floor of our cider operation, the flood had deposited a foot and a half of wet silt.

"But think how lucky we are," Rick said when we got back to the house. "This could have happened today, after we had set up everything."

"That's true," I said.

"Couldn't you press right here on the front porch?" Gayle suggested.

Rick and I considered her offer. There was an electric outlet for the grinder and pump. And at the end of the porch was a water tap. We could do it. We pressed on the porch for a week until the silt dried out in the tractor shed and we could move in there.

Every day that we weren't pressing and weren't at market, we picked apples. Sometimes we did not start pressing until afternoon and finished at night and cleaned racks by flashlight outside. I would leave Rick to handle the cleanup, and I'd get up at five the next morning to go to market. By the time I would get home he would have already been picking for several hours.

We picked our orchard, and we picked many other unsprayed orchards all the way to the Tesuque Valley, almost to Santa Fe. The last apples we harvested in the snow, in November, in La Bolsa, a little orchard by the Rio Grande.

And everything we pressed had to be sold immediately. In that season we had cider in three stores in Santa Fe, one in Los Alamos, and three in Taos. I went to Tuesday market at Santa Fe, Thursday market at Los Alamos, and Saturday market at Santa Fe. Sometimes Rick and I went together. At the end of the season I added everything up; in this, our first full year of pressing, we had made and sold two thousand gallons of cider.

The next year I laid a slab of cement across the front half of the shed. We had plenty of apples, so Rick took off the fall semester to help press. We pushed each other—to find more apples, to press more cider, to find more customers. And we bested our first year by two hundred gallons. Come November we were both exhausted.

It was our last season making cider together, and that record for gallons pressed and sold still stands. No one but a family member would have worked with me as hard and long for as little pay and with such unflagging good humor. But I wish for the cidermaster-to-come an apprentice, related by blood or not, such as I had in Rick.

GAYLE AND I pull weeds from between the green beans and the purple beans and the corn and the tomatoes and carry them in great armfuls to the ducks and the geese and the chickens. I look up and catch the piñon and juniper stealing their way up the hill toward the television antenna and Father Meyers's cross, the new dispensation and the old. They freeze in place, among the sage and the fragile patches of grass, pretending they were not going anywhere. But I know better; when I turn away they will keep climbing until they reach the top, like everything else, the summit or die. And I look higher, to the rock face of La Mesita beyond, where we have climbed, where we found the lava collapse cave and the rattlesnake and saw the eagle. I scan the green and brown and then the blue and the white, forms and values changing every moment.

The tall weeds have delicate leaves like mimosa that belie their fruit, the brown burrs. I pull one, two, three and then give up counting. I reach the patch of bindweed, wild morning glory. Yes, I admire the fine, red penstemon-like blossom as well as the traditional blue petunia-like blossom. I play no favorites. Out! Out! I pull another vine. It breaks. I reach down between the plants to find the root. And again, and again, for with bindweed the end is not near. It will survive us along with the locust.

And here is the purslane feeling its way across the ground. I bite the leaves from the first pull. A bit sour, like spinach with lemon. We pull purslane, lamb's quarters, too, along with the grasses and sandburs and so many others I recognize but cannot name. We pull them all, and release corn and squash and cucumbers and chile peppers.

Tomorrow is my birthday. I will go to the farmers' market in Santa Fe with more apricots, plums, summer apples, and whatever else I can think of. Right now I cannot think of anything. Nephews Ben and Aaron left for home yesterday. Gayle put them on the plane for Salt Lake City in Albuquerque. They had offered us three weeks of help, but we felt we had to pay them something, and the tickets cost ninety-eight dollars each. That took a big chunk out of what we earned in three weeks of farmers' markets in Los Alamos and Santa Fe.

But the apricots have to be picked. I cannot look at thirty trees and more covered with yellow and orange and orange-red fruit and not pick. Even if Los Alamos and Santa Fe are swimming in apricots? The farmer has to pick, whether or not he can find a market. At least that is the guidance I have given myself. Still the ground is covered with what the boys and I have not picked. And more will come.

THURSDAY, SEPTEMBER 20th, 9:30 A.M., Los Alamos market. "The Plant Lady," as she calls herself, comes up with her arms full of nursery catalogs and gardening and farming magazines. She waits for the appropriate moment between customers and then starts.

"Here's an article about disease-free apples." She hands me *National Gardening*, the gardener's newsmagazine, with a cluster of apples on the cover. "Here's one about old-fashioned apple varieties." She hands me *Organic Gardening*. "Here's a list of nurseries that sell old-fashioned apples. And here's Miller's catalog; they sell old-fashioned apples. And here's—"

"I have that one," I say.

"Isn't it interesting?" she says. "Now be sure to get these back to me. Maybe you can Xerox the list and send for the catalogs."

I thank her and set the stack on the tailgate as she walks away. When I first met this woman, she was acting as market manager. She went from vendor to vendor checking for conformity to the rules established by county and state health regulators: all produce must be at least twelve inches off the ground, no uninspected jams or salsas or baked goods, no dairy products, and so on. And there was a heaviness about her approach; instead of a lighthearted manner that could ease conformity, hers was an enforcing approach that might raise resistance in farmers who were already stressed by hard work and the long hours of a market day. Policing was not this woman's skill, and now I realize it might not be her real interest either. She is a horticulturist. She has information. And we had talked about the old apples in our orchard—I vaguely remember that.

I pick up the stack of magazines and catalogs from the tail-gate. The sheer weight makes me feel even more tired than usual on a market day. You pick and sort fruit till dark, stay up late loading the truck, then get up at four-thirty or five to drive to market. And then you drive home very carefully, with the window wide-open, remembering the farmer driving home from the Los Alamos market, falling asleep, turning into the hillside, and barely escaping with her life. And the routine goes on and on till November. I put these reading materials inside the truck. Someday I might have time to look through them, but that is not a high priority in this season.

11 A.M. A break in customers, and I walk down the road.

"Hi, how are you?" Two women, my age, from Chimayo, call me over. Cucumbers, beans, tomatoes, green and white squash laid out on a tablecloth. Last week I was parked next to them. "Where are you today?"

"Up the road," and I point behind me. "Good-looking toma-toes," I say. "Are you doing all right?"

"A little slow. And you?"

"The same," and I smile.

Next to them Sophie has two customers, so I just wave. It's good to see her up; she had an operation earlier in the season.

Then blue-eyed Abel Martinez in a cowboy hat and polished boots comes out from behind his baskets of polished apples and neat stacks of red chile powder in clear plastic bags and accosts me. "Hey, I'm glad to see you! I went to the bank yesterday, and they turned me down. How about a loan?" He grins and his wife standing behind him laughs.

"I was just going to ask you the same thing," I say. "And how's the water coming?"

"Sit down here and I'll tell you about it."

"Later," I say. "Good luck!" and I walk on. I have sympathized with Abel's problems with a tough acequia commission, and I will listen again when I can. Now I want to go through the whole market, before things get too busy, to see who's here and what they have. I may buy something Gayle needs, or maybe swap for it at the end of the day, when growers often have surplus to exchange or give away. And should a customer ask me today where to find sweet peas or yellow squash, I may actually know.

For farmers the market is a community. And some things we understand without talking about, like childhood friends who have gone to the same schools and played sandlot games together. We all know about la jara, and la limpia, cutting the willows and cleaning the acequia in the spring. We all know about drought years when you get out at two in the morning for your turn to water. And we all know that our New Mexico is not like ancient Egypt, with seven fat years and seven lean. A good harvest may be followed by another good harvest, or a poor one, or no harvest at all. We farm because we want to and because we can. And we tell each other stories. My favorite is the one about the old farmer who won a million dollars in the lottery. A reporter came out to do a feature for the weekly paper. "Congratulations, sir, you won the lottery! Now what are you planning to do?"

The old farmer looked around at his place, the tired house and barn, the well-used tractor and pickup, the field he had just plowed. He was quiet for a minute. Then he said, with a smile, "I guess I'll just keep on farming until all the money is gone."

At the Los Alamos market we park our pickups and set up our boxes and tables under great ponderosa pines in a city park. The dirt road curves around the trees, and the trucks and vans back up to it on both sides, each taking as much space as he needs. Those who come earliest get the best spots, in the shade of the big trees. Latecomers get more sun. But there is always space. Officially this market ends at noon, but farmers can stay longer to sell to people who cannot get away during regular market hours.

Santa Fe, with five times the population of Los Alamos, does farmers' markets Tuesdays and Saturdays in a tree-lined parking lot with numbered, reserved spaces. You must be in your space by

6:30, and close by 11:30. A midseason Saturday market is usually packed with growers from all the northern counties and local buyers and visitors from everywhere. It's like a country fair, a street concert, a block party, and a European market all rolled into one. People line up for plates of salads and bowls of soup from city chefs using local produce. Down the rows they pick up berries and grapes, slices of apple, pear, peach, and melon, bites of hot chile, tastes of chile jam and sweet jam, and cups of fresh cider. The fiddler and the banjo player stop at the entrance, sing about the farmers and the mountains in Spanish and English, then move to another space and sing other songs, or the same ones again. A visitor stops at a flower grower, sees color, red and purple and yellow colors he expects alongside new colors just invented this year. He lifts his camera. And again and again as he walks down the aisle. A visitor from Japan follows with a video camera. And at the far end of the market, the distinctly New Mexican experience of roasting chile demands one more shot— green chile spinning to black in the gas-fired roasting drum.

SANTA FE market. Saturday morning, 6:45 A.M., the asphalt parking lot behind Sanbusco Center, within walking distance of the old Santa Fe Plaza. Early fall. Every space is filled, more than eighty sellers: local growers of every traditional and uncommon variety of fruit and vegetable and flower that can survive the northern New Mexico climate; producers of preserves, baked goods, eggs, apple cider, lamb and mutton, goat cheese, teas, herbal remedies and soaps, wreaths and ristras; and crafters of the practical and the decorative made from what is locally grown or gathered. We are here, in place, setting up, arranging, displaying, making signs. Many of us have gotten up at four to drive in from the northern or eastern counties. The melon grower leaves his farm at two-thirty in the morning. And some harvested and loaded their trucks till late Friday, after doing fieldwork all week and perhaps also coming to Tuesday market here and going to Thursday market in Los Alamos. But the farmer's fatigue doesn't matter; the market opens in fifteen minutes, and early shoppers are already walking in.

Next to me, halfway down the first aisle, Rose Mary Crawford carries long ristras of garlic from the truck to the display board. She walks between her bushel baskets of multicolor bouquets, plump bouquets of tiny statice blossoms, the magical flower already dry when you pick it.

Stan Crawford sets a tub of fresh basil on the board that serves as his counter, next to a tub of leeks and another of shallots.

Jan Barbo across the way carries cut flowers out of her truck, some in bouquets, some singles, puts them into vases and jars and cans on her tables and on the ground. Next to her the sprout man takes trays of sunflower and radish sprouts out of the trunk of his car and sets them on two bridge tables.

Truman Brigham, next to the sprout man, stands in the middle of a perimeter of produce, a rectangle with three sides, wooden boxes set up on steel milk crates and the fourth side the tailgate of his pickup. Green squash, yellow squash, tomatoes, apples, carrots with their tops, turnips, chard, pears, raspberries, lettuce, spinach—all planted and grown and then picked last night by him and his helpers. Truman is seventy-five. He looks too thin in his faded brown shirt and brown pants; his face is sun and wind blasted, and his nose is peeling. He has been farming in New Mexico for fifty years and coming to the Santa Fe market since its beginning—and he will continue coming to market for ten more years until his daughter drives him to the hospital and he moves on to the great truck farm in the sky.

Next to Truman, Jim Gilbert and his son Kevin and daughter, Xahra, set up a homemade sun awning and two tables under it. Now they unload the jars of chili and pesto and chutney, condiments Jim and Camille and their children make at their farm in Rio Oscuro, the next farm up the highway from ours. Jim and I were born in the same month in the same year. We both spent years in Europe and had European first wives. Besides being a farmer and condiment innovator, and also a painter, Jim is an aficionado of wild mushrooming, and has graciously shared trea-sured spots with Gayle and me.

Next to the Gilberts, Angelina Valdez unloads baskets of giant apples and boxes of ordinary apples and peaches from her family farm in the next village south of Rio Oscuro. It was Angelina who identified our large grapefruit-size apples as Wolf River and the large pink-and-whites as Maidenblush. I enjoy pronouncing her name in the Spanish way, the *g* like our *h*, Anhe-leéna.

Across from her, back on my side of the walkway, Ana Mae Salazar lays on her tables wreaths of dried flowers so intricate they look woven on a loom. Next to them her mother-in-law sets out baskets of apples and peaches and plums, and her brother-in-law opens sacks of green chile and heaps sweet corn on another table.

All day Friday Rose Mary and her helpers had worked with the garlic and the tiny blue, white, yellow, chocolate-brown, or-ange, purple, and tan blossoms of statice; tying; combining colors and wrapping; loading the truck; then helping Stan harvest basil, lettuce, shallots, turnips, and onions; then cleaning the greens and onions; packing them; loading the truck; getting to bed late before getting up at four for the drive to market, to be here by six-fifteen, to unload and set up. And, with minor variations, the Crawfords' story is Jan Barbo's story, the Gilberts' story, Truman's story, Angelina's story, Ana Mae's story, Jake West's story (who leaves at 2:30 to truck his melons all the way from Fort Sumner), and my story.

People are already taking bunches of basil, weighing shallots, handing money to Stan. I catch the strong green smell of basil as it wafts from Stan and Rose Mary's space over the first shoppers and into the early morning air. Across the way Jan and her daugh-ter set out more cut flowers on her tables and on the ground. Now her space is a mass of reds, and golds, and purples. In between are heaps of pears and baskets of raspberries. I wave, she calls back. Two women stop. More people, men and women in run-ning shorts, women and men in brightly colored sweats, men and women with environmentally conscious canvas and net shopping bags. Still ten minutes to opening.

My display table faces the walkway. I have stacked open boxes of apples and pears and grapes along the sides of my space with small signs indicating variety and price. The scale is on the table. Recycled bags, paper and plastic, are in a box. Now I put all the cider that is not in coolers, about thirty half-gallons, on the table, turning their black-and-red "Big Willow" labels to the front. I glance across the way. There's Truman lifting another box of greens out of his truck. He sets this box in the last opening in his display along the border of his eight-by-ten space. As usual he is the first vendor to arrive and to be set up. Now he stands by the tailgate, looking around. I watch him. He catches me. He crosses over, stands in front of my table.

"Hello, Truman! How are you?"

"Hello, Harvey." His voice is slow, his eyes moist behind his glasses. "Do you suppose I could have a little of your good cider? My throat is awful dry."

"Of course." I take a bottle and twist off the red plastic safety cap. I pour into a one-ounce plastic sample cup, fill it as full as I can. "That's the only kind of cup I have." I hold the cup out. As he takes it in his dark-veined hand I see a slight tremble. A few drops spill as he lifts the cup to his lips. He drinks it all. "Want more?"

"That's fine. Thanks, Harvey."

I smile and nod. "Anytime, Truman." It's an honor to serve this man.

"And you come over and get whatever you want." And he walks back to his space where the first customers are holding greens for him to price.

9:30. I HAVE poured a hundred tastes of cider, sliced apples and pears and peaches, offered Father Meyers's Niagara, Carmine, and Concord grapes to a dozen samplers. Most of the cider is gone, all the peaches, and half the grapes and pounds and pounds of apples and pears.

And of the people I know besides other farmers, I see more in these two and a half hours than I see in a month on the farm. Pamela of Seranata de Santa Fe who seems born to play the oboe whenever we hear her, with her four-year-old son who likes our fruit and our cider; Victor, the public health doctor who birthed the New Mexico Men's Wellness Conference and wrote a book on stopping violence and brings his daughters to the farm to help harvest apples; and Sam, Trevor's adopted grandpa who has become part of our family: that's three of so many today. We say how are you, how have you been, and smile, and that is all, for there's always someone standing behind asking which apples are good for pies, or whether Carmine grapes are like Concords, or what's the cider blend this week, or can they order a case of cider for next week. And I am here to attend to these questions. One to one, grower to buyer, what our farmers' market is all about.

A tap on the shoulder. It's Juan, Juan Velasco who helped make this cider two days ago. We embrace in the style of men's wellness and of Bolivia where he grew up, a strong embrace with both arms, man to man. He sits down on the tailgate beside me.

"Can I get you some coffee, or a scone?" Juan, always gracious and generous. Maybe later, I say. But for now would he mind watching the shop? I am filled with market; I need a little walk.

THE LINE between apple cider and art begins to blur toward the end of the market season. Fellow artists, old friends, and collectors of Gayle's watercolors pick up their jugs of cider and ask how she's doing and when is this year's Rio Oscuro Studio Tour. In October I put a stack of art-tour maps beside the cider. The tour is always the first weekend in November, and Gayle paints toward it all summer and fall. Thirty other artists and artisans on the tour, including Jim Gilbert and Rose Mary and Stan, also prepare their works and their farms and studios weeks and months in advance. Eight thousand maps are printed, and thousands of visitors and buyers show up, from all over New Mexico, from Texas, Colorado, and Arizona, and some from the Midwest, the East Coast, and the West Coast.

THE STUDIO tour starts at nine Saturday morning, and promptly at nine this Saturday the first vehicle rolls up the driveway. All the signs are up, and I'm just finishing the feeding and watering of the geese and ducks, who will not be allowed out on this day. I wave. I recognize the three women as friends of Gayle's and long-time supporters and collectors. They always come early; they want first pick. By the time I come up to the house, one woman is already carrying a painting down the stone stairway to their car.

The mulled cider steams in the blue enamel kettle on the warm gray woodstove inside the gallery. I catch the smell as I open the door. Five people are already in the gallery. I offer hot cider. Four takers. I pour, serve. More people come in. In the studio two people are standing by Gayle with paintings. She is talking to a man I recognize from El Paso, a doctor. Has he come all this way this morning? Later I find out he and his wife stayed overnight in Santa Fe. I help those waiting, calculate the tax, cut bubble wrap for protection, tape it together. More people. Last year it rained on Saturday. The year before it snowed. Today the sun is shining. More cars arrive. Rick helps them park. Some people park on the paved road and walk. Part of the pleasure of the tour, they say, is parking by the river and walking by the orchard and the grapes and the birds and the big willows up to Gayle's studio.

At the end of the day, before we turn off the lights, I look at the empty spaces on the walls of the gallery and the studio. "People really like what you do," I say.

Gayle smiles. It has been a good day, yet greeting almost a thousand people and talking with a hundred at least has been very tiring. And this is just Saturday. Tomorrow there will be more. But this is what the artist works for and hopes for—that people will come to see and appreciate the paintings she has put so much of herself into, and then take paintings home to become part of their lives.

IN NOVEMBER 1990, after the end of the cider season, Marni came up to the farm to help Gayle with the annual Rio Oscuro Studio Tour. That fall Marni had decided to go back to graduate school at the University of New Mexico. We saw her whenever we visited Albuquerque; she came to the farm when her schedule permitted, and over the years she wove her life into the cycles and seasons of the farm. When Marni came she took on what to others might seem the worst of tasks: pruning the tangle of Father Meyers's vineyard, repainting the narrow wooden mullions on old ten-pane glass doors, and repelling the invasion of tent caterpillars. Almost overnight the caterpillars had webbed themselves into the big orchard. Everywhere I turned black larvae wiggled and wriggled inside filmy gray shrouds covering great branches. We knew that burning them out was the answer, and Marni offered to do it. She was out the whole day with newspaper torches, and when she came in all the caterpillars were gone.

Marni knew, of course, how important the weekend of the studio tour was for us. Three to four thousand people came from Albuquerque and Santa Fe to visit the studios, workshops, and farms in and around the village. Gayle might earn half our annual income in art sales over the weekend. But it snowed and rained that Saturday in 1990, and by afternoon when Marni arrived the lowest part of the road along the orchard was a slough that visitors did not want to cross. She and I got long-handled shovels from the stone barn. We dug a ditch to drain the water into the orchard and then started throwing dirt into the low spot. We worked and we laughed. This wasn't exactly what I had in mind, I said, when I used to tell her she could do anything she put her mind to.

"I never know what I'll get into when I come up here," she said. "It's always something interesting."

It was after five when we finished. There were no more tourists that day. But the road would be passable on Sunday.

Despite the snow and rain, the day had been busy for Gayle. We were all tired. Marni baked cookies and nut cakes for Sunday, told us stories of professors and exams, and went to bed. The sun came out the next morning, and the people who had put off coming came, along with those who had planned a Sunday visit. A steady stream of lookers and buyers and old patrons and friends, hundreds and hundreds, maybe a thousand. In the middle of the afternoon Marni introduced me to a young man named Peter, a young man just her age, a young man from Pittsburgh visiting a friend in Santa Fe. It turned out that Sam, Peter's host, knew a close friend of Gayle's. Sam had learned about the Rio Oscuro tour from the mutual friend and for years had talked about going; Peter's visit made this the year. I shook hands with Peter and wished him a good time in New Mexico.

A week later, now the middle of November, Gayle and I went to Albuquerque to exhibit her work at the Southwest Arts Festival. We took Marni to lunch, to thank her for coming up to help at the art tour and to celebrate her thirtieth birthday. She glowed. "I met the man I'm going to marry."

I looked at her and smiled; I didn't know what to say. Gayle, always a little more present, said that was very good. Who was he? "I met him at the farm! I introduced you to him! Peter Keegan!" Gayle did remember him and her Santa Fe friend's friend Sam, and, happily, I remembered, too.

"He's wonderful," she said. "And Dad, Peter's birthday is the same as yours!" I learned later of the hand weather had played in this meeting, that Sam and Peter had started out from Santa Fe on Saturday morning to go to the tour, but they turned back because of the snow and came Sunday instead. Marni didn't come until late Saturday afternoon. Without the snow, how would Marni and Peter have met?

PART 2

The Study of Ice

Winter is the time for
another look and another chance.
THE CIDERMASTER'S HANDBOOK

OUR RIVER BEGINS as snowmelt and runoff in the highest
mountain range of northern New Mexico. One August we hiked
to its source at San Leonardo Lakes eleven thousand feet high in
the Pecos Wilderness, and there was still snow across from a bank
of wildflowers. Seven tributaries bring the thaw and the summer
rains down from the Sangre de Cristos: Rio La Junta, Rio del
Pueblo, Rio Santa Barbara, Rio Chiquito, Rio Las Trampas, and
Rito Ojo Sarco. They wind in and out of wooded canyons. They
water pueblo and Spanish pastures and fields and orchards in
chains of narrow valleys that lead to the Rio Grande. Above the
last of these valleys the waters become what we know as el Rio
Oscuro. Our orchard lies on a north slope in this last valley, and
our acequia is the final one to draw water from the Oscuro.

Living on a north-facing slope has taught me most of what I
know about ice. We can count on a solid month of ice almost
every year; in some years, two and even three months. The south
slope opposing us may seem almost balmy with its ice all but
vanished by the middle of February. In mild winters, south-slope

apples can bloom in March. If we are lucky, the cold and shade will hold back our trees from blossoming long enough for the fruit to miss the killing May frost. But here my topic is not the farmer's lament. It is ice. My study begins with the new year, the beginning of January.

Ice: ice crusts that I break as I go through the upper orchard to the pole barn, and that the horses break as they come into the narrow pasture to meet me and wait for their hay; melted ice on the road, ice on snow that stops the car halfway up the drive, so Gayle must come out to steer while I push and we navigate together around the turns and up the hill and into the shed; tiny pockets and flaps and covers and laces of ice where the snow has melted back under the stiff vines and around the trunks and in the fence corners; icicles, of course, hanging from the eaves, crystal picks longer than my arms, sharp and shining, appearing overnight after days of solid cold; roof ice, not icicles but long bars of ice edging the great sheets of snow that slide down the roof and harden into cornices; window ice, the magical hoarfrost we remember from childhood; and, finally, the indomitable ice, the ice that returns every morning no matter how many afternoons and evenings I break it and dump it out, the ice that never gives up: bucket ice.

MANY DAYS I have walked down this road. In the fall, in the dark and hopeful early morning, I carry my steaming breakfast omelet and toast and tea down to the truck loaded with fruit and cider for the farmers' market. In the early spring I carry the bucket full of warm water down to the laying hens, sidestepping, going around the mud, and then slipping and slopping water on myself. I go down in the silent moonlight, in the silent rain, in the absolute, silent heat on the first of August, my birthday. And this road to the fall market and the spring chickens, to hoeing corn and picking peaches and smelling honeysuckle, is also the road to chopping ice.

The shape and thickness of ice in the water buckets tells me more about the outside temperature than the thermometer on the front porch. Today the overnight cold has frozen the ducks' water into a block so thick that no amount of my chopping with the steel pipe can break through. But I keep chopping, because there is nothing else to do. Finally, pipe finds water—just as it punctures the side of the bucket. Oh. I put down the pipe. This is a reinforced, freeze-resistant, all-weather bucket. Gayle bought me this bucket last year, after I punched a hole in the dog pail, battered and bent the roasting pan till it would never again hold turkey or water, and then backed the van over the one last, good galvanized bucket we owned. This new bucket was expensive because it was both heavy and flexible and would not crack in the cold. Yet there it lies, pierced, useless. I have to find another way.

UNCLE BILL does not understand why we are studying ice. "I could not begin to undertake the things you speak about in your letter. Why have you chosen such a hard path?" he writes. In truth New York knows much more of winter than New Mexico. But for Uncle Bill, the winter so real to him in the cold-water flat of his childhood has now become part of the great out-there, that which lies behind the page, behind the screen, the white and not even white grayness beyond his sixteenth-story apartment window.

I can understand my uncle's question. Dividing the world between out-there, which includes everything in the past and everything in the present beyond our touch, and our separate, individual in-here is so common that we think of it as the natural process for our species and all others. My problem is that this separation that the city promotes makes me feel caged. But can I survive outside the cage? My grandfather went to the city as a young man. My father spent his whole life in cities. I grew up in a city. City breeding has given me hands and fingers that are almost too small for farmwork. As I work the wheelbarrow and the hoe and the hammer my fingers seem to outgrow my hands until I cannot make a fist without a finger popping out of its socket. So have I come back to earth, to learn the earth all over again. I will make it. I have made my choice.

IN DECEMBER, two days before he went back to Idaho, Joshua, our nephew and sometime live-in cider helper, chased away an owl from the guinea pen. I don't usually attend to guinea screams anymore. It's when they are quiet that I might be concerned. But Josh heard them and ran out, and there was the owl on the chicken wire above the doorway, either trying to get in or trying to get out. It wasn't a giant, he said, not much bigger than a guinea. But what wings! It took off like a shot, and disappeared up the hill.

He looked inside and counted—still six guineas and the four Brahman roosters. The wire was loose, though; the owl could have gotten in.

"Can you fix it?" I asked.

"I can staple it; that should work."

The next day I went to inspect the guinea pen myself. I looked for loose wire, for an opening big enough for an owl. The top of the frame was black, rotted, barely hanging on to the nail in the side piece, which itself was only a little less rotted. It was not so much the wire that was loose as the whole doorway. Any self-respecting owl could probably knock the whole thing in if it so desired, if it were cold enough and hungry enough. There was nothing loose about the wire that was not true of the whole pen.

It was make-do, to get us through the winter. Normally the guineas would be outside, roosting in the trees. And that's what they were doing until one by one they started disappearing. Coyotes again, yet we had not seen any for a month. Maybe the neighbor's chows? Then Josh found a headless guinea in the black walnut tree. Just hanging there, where the birds had been roosting.

"What could have done that?" he asked.

"A raccoon?"

"Why would a raccoon leave the bird, not take it away?"

So we brought the guineas up to the old pen by the house, the one without a door. We cut chicken wire to cover the entry. Now, stapled on one side and hooked over nails on the other, it made a poor door, yet still a protection enough from the owl.

Protection. Over the years what has our protection spared? Not the guinea hen who walked twelve of her fifteen day-old chicks to their demise in the acequia. Not the five ducklings who floated down the acequia and never came back. Not the geese or roosters or hens or guineas or ducks or cats taken by the coyotes.

When a bird disappears I do not want to look for it. I have found more than one heap of feathers on the first mesa above the acequia. The ducks parade up the walk, past the studio, past the front porch, then jump in the acequia and swim down again. They get into the flowers and the strawberries. Sometimes they have walked right into the kitchen when the door was open. I feel a kinship with them; I do not want to find them dead. But that will happen, whatever our precautions.

ALMOST EVERYTHING on this farm is susceptible to improvement. The duck-pen door is a flimsy patchwork of weathered wood and chicken wire. It functions; it opens and closes, and it keeps the ducks in. If my nails and baling wire have done nothing to improve its appearance, at least they have not interfered with these functions. Now as I try to open the door, the bottom hinge comes apart. I bend down to look for the pin. But the ducks are watching. They boister toward the opening, announcing each thrust of hip and foot with the duck battle cry, a great quacking armada of waddling bills and feathers. Perhaps they think it is summer again and I am letting them out to swim in the ditch, or nibble grass on the bank, or parade down the walk, or wander down the lane to the garden. Well, whatever they think, I put my boot in their path. The sun is warm, but we turned the ditch off months ago. It is winter, coyote season. Not a good time for ducks to be cavorting in arroyos or on ditch banks or along hidden paths.

The hinge pin is in the dirt, just where I found it a week ago when it fell out the first time and I discovered that this hinge, like several others in the house, had been mounted upside down. Actually, that discovery was a relief; at first I thought that the hinge had broken, that I would have to take time out to find some kind of replacement, probably replace the door, and maybe the whole front wall, because the doorpost has completely rotted away in the moist, muddy duckness and the wall now swings from the beam whenever I move the door. But all I have to do now is put the pin back again.

I ease the door into place, wood to rotting wood and metal to rusting metal. I hold the pin to the hinge, and push, push as hard as I can—but today it will not go in.

All right. Maybe this is the time to undertake an improvement, to align myself with the tribe of fixers. Their philosophy has been explained to me more than once, and I have listened carefully, even admiringly. I have always left their presence with respect for their energy and commitment, and have continued muddling to another drummer.

I set the door into the frame, close the hasp, and put back the bent nail. The ducks holler at me: Never mind the door! Let us out! Feed! Water!! Now, now, now!!! No, I do not listen. If I stopped every time a duck hollered there would not be a door left on its hinges or a wall still standing. I need tools. I head for the stone barn ten steps away.

The first time we opened the barn door we confronted a solid waist-high mass of newspapers, magazines, catalogs, folded and flattened milk cartons, feed sacks, plastic bags, paper bags, boxes of pleated paper cups that once held chocolates, jars and bottles of all sizes, cardboard, string, rope, rubber bands, an old doghouse, rusted springs, shoes, boots, rusted nails, screws, glass. There was more of the same on the shelves and in the loft. Across the debris we could see the back wall and the top of what looked like a door. What was behind the door? And how did all this stuff get here? There was no one to ask.

Fifty years ago the parishioners of Iglesia San Ysidro shoveling and picking into this hill may have believed they were building a garage for Father Meyers's car, just as they believed it was their duty to give their priest this service. Certainly there is depth enough for his old Buick touring car. And the dirt floor, the walls of earth and rock, the massive vigas, peeled but neither painted nor stained, the ceiling of rough, uneven planks, and the big double doors—these were the makings of a garage. Of course, no other farm in the village had such a great rock and earth garage. But then no other was owned by a village priest from Germany.

How long did the stone barn house the touring car? Many of the artifacts we could logically associate with the priest, but I do not know whether he put them there or whether his housekeepers began the great accumulation after his death. Toward the end of the household, with Victoria in her nineties, ailing, and rarely able to leave the house, and only Corina, in her seventies, still getting out to the chickens and ducks and rabbits, I can imagine "We'll save this, Corina," as a last ritual between them.

"All right, Victoria," and Corina would head out. She would put her key into the tiny padlock, pull back the hasp, and open the right-hand door. Now she would lift whatever she was carrying to shoulder height and throw it as far as she could into the depths. Finally, she would push the door shut, relock it, and report back: "It is done."

Yet the evidence tells a different story. Not all the accumulation was debris. The bits of string and yarns and ribbon balled and tied, the pieces of fabric bagged and boxed, the boxes of beads and folded Christmas wrappings and piles of silks from old cigarette packages, and the jars and jars of seeds with their penciled notations—"french cantaloupe from Mr. Grant, very sweet, 1976"; "big tomatoes, 1973"; "Italian squash, 1969"; "special cucumbers, 1977"—these were things of value stowed away with care against an uncertain future, perhaps, as in a pharaoh's tomb, for a use beyond time.

A month after we arrived a man from the village asked if we had found the buried treasure. We laughed. He was serious. There was treasure buried on our place. What or where he did not know, nor did he say how people living in this run-down, impoverished place ever accrued any treasure worth burying. But people in Rio Oscuro knew about Father Meyers's and Victoria's treasure, he said, and he stood by it.

Gayle and I considered the possibility of there being some kind of buried treasure. If it existed, and we found it, that would be a big help. But neither of us had any idea where to look. Then Gayle thought of that door at the end of the garage, behind that mass of stuff. Treasure hunting was not our top priority, but the door in the garage stayed in the backs of our minds. Sometimes, at night, we asked each other what we would do if there really were a treasure, somewhere, out there.

Months passed before we had the time to work on the garage and clear out enough stuff so we could get to the back. At last the day came when we could open the mystery door. Inside was what used to be a small room dug into the hill. Now it was almost completely filled with dirt that had sifted in through the boards in the ceiling and sloughed off from the earthen walls. All we could see above the dirt was the wooden top of what looked like an old wine barrel. We climbed over the dirt, and I lifted the cover. It came apart in my hand. We looked inside. The light was too dim to see much, but what we did see was the inside of a barrel filled with empty wine bottles. I turned to Gayle.

"Are you disappointed?"

"Not really. I wasn't expecting anything." And even if there were a treasure somewhere, it could hide forever under the mountains of silt.

I pulled a bottle out of the barrel, and Gayle looked at it. "Maybe these old bottles are worth something."

I glance now at tools I have hung on the wall—a crosscut saw, a crowbar, a nail puller. I ask myself how far I want to go with this repair. I take my favorite hammer, the straight-jawed Plumb with its red fiberglass handle. I take some four-penny nails. Small hinge, small nails. The ducks start in again as soon as I come back. "What's the matter? Where's our water? You're keeping us waiting! Waiting! Kwa-kwa-kwah! Kwa-kwa-kwah!" I set the door in the hinge, hold it with my shoulder, stick in the pin, and tap it up. Now I hold a nail under the pin, and tap the nail. The weathered wood does not split. I hit the nail again, and again, until the head is all the way under the head of the hinge pin. I stand up. It is a fix: the old nail-pin trick favored by those of us who live with upside-down hinges. Now for the ducks.

SATURDAY, THE twentieth of January. At seven this morning the snow has left, and fog envelops the white trees and fences, the white trucks, the white cider house, and all the white peaks and the white mesas across the river. The fog holds the valley in, keeps it apart from whatever lies without. As I move down the road through the fog-filtered light, I am like a wraith, casting no shadow. I seem to float. I feel no gravity. My footprints in the snow are part of a game I play or not, at my choice.

The chickens, who have barely tolerated the snow this winter, now stay close to their house. Some do not come out at all. But the ducks and geese have no compunctions. As soon as I open their door, they rush into the snow and gobble it down. They are more thirsty than hungry.

The horses wait under the great Bartlett pear tree. Their backs are streaked with ribbons of ice. Finally I get the red pan with oats, squeeze between the gatepost and the fence, and start down toward the barn. Both horses are with me immediately, trying to sniff up some oats over my shoulder. I elbow them out of the way, but they keep coming. At the barn they go into the feeding stalls, and I go into the center where we keep the hay.

It is not that cold; I decide they can make do with a plug and a half each this morning. I push the plugs through the opening and divide the feed, half to the right and half to the left. Groaner has stopped at the far-right stall this time.

"Groaner!" He does not move. "Here's your feed, Groaner." Still he does not move. Finally I go out. I shove him, "Go!" At last he moves, past Xeno and into his own spot. Now I go back into the barn and pour the oats on the hay, to the right and to the left.

When I look again it is nine-thirty, time to go for the mail.

The fog is lifting. By eleven the sun is out in full force, and the new snow begins to melt. After lunch I hang out the clothes that Gayle has washed. The sun is bright; some things should dry today. The clothesline pole is now above the house, and I am surrounded by juniper and piñon that run up the top of our hill where the cross Victoria had erected in memory of Father Meyers and the television antenna she had erected sometime later both reach toward heaven.

I pin a corner of the blue bottom sheet to the highest line, then fold it back so it does not touch the ground. Dark green trees, snow-covered rocks, and blue bedsheet. Blue sheet on the hill, snow in the valley, bare branches of cottonwoods along the river, bare branches of apple trees in our orchard and the neighbor's orchard to the west. And now just patches of snow on the south slope of the mountain across the river. Cars run up the river highway, and cars run down, fast, as though there never had been a snow today, and never a fog. The finches sing around me. This is their kind of weather—a little snow gives a piquancy to the seeds, the berries, and the grain they steal from the guinea pen. This is their time of year, so long as they stay sharp and away from the cats and coyotes.

I finish hanging the clothes. I feel a shadow, look up. More clouds are coming in from the west. Maybe there will be more snow tonight. With luck, another fog early Sunday morning. I go in. I can still hear the finches, and the water dripping off the roof and into the shallow tub, the tub where the ducks play in the summer and the dogs drink all year when it is not frozen. And if there is no fog tomorrow, that will be just right, too.

ON THE farm winter has always been my time for second looks and second chances. We had made a lot of good cider, and people liked it. But that was done, and this was January, a new year. I did not wonder how much cider we should make the next year. Although Rick had moved to Albuquerque at the beginning of January and had now enrolled at the University of New Mexico, and I would need a new helper, I still thought we should press as much as we possibly could. I had the view that because you can do something, you should do it. If it was two thousand gallons last time, then do at least that much the next time, and more if possible.

The problems with weather I dismissed in the same fashion. It seldom rains hard enough for the arroyo to run, and even if it did run, it could hurt us only if we were working outside. I thought that by observing nature, in this case the weather, by interpreting its processes, and then by integrating them into my way of life I would be in control.

Note my foolishness. Controlling nature is an illusion. We are controlled rather than controlling. And the harder we try to control natural forces, the more serious are the consequences we experience. And when we make superhuman efforts, try to make our fruit bug-proof, and our lives flood-proof, fireproof, depression-proof, radiation-proof, or bomb- and missile-proof, the inevitable consequence, however long the delay, is catastrophe. But these will not be revelations for the cidermaster yet to come. He will know all about the perils of arrogance and about caring for his living orchards.

The working conditions Rick and I had endured had been terrible, and clearly we would have to move the operation inside before the next season. That meant cleaning out the old wine-making and storage shed. It was another pastoral reliquary left behind by Father Meyers and his housekeepers: the gallons and gallons of wine gone bad, the boxes upon boxes of apples dried out and rotten in narrow stalls made of scrap wood, the litter, the broken tables, the old icebox. And more in the next room: old peach baskets, egg cartons, bundles of newspapers, basket lids, feed sacks, rusted cans of rusted nails, a heap of lead pipe and valves and faucets, the broken bedspring, the unopened and opened bottles and boxes and cans of fertilizers and agricultural poisons, and tacked to the wall and the doorpost old calendars with penciled records of egg production for each day of the year. Gayle and I and her young nephews had made a start hauling out the wasted apples a year ago. But much more had to be hauled away and then the wooden stalls dismantled and the crooked, dirty lumber hauled outside before I could even think of improvements.

The great dirt-floored wine-making room with its high, pitched ceiling—a room as large as a small beach house, actually—must have been a center of activity on this farm. I can imagine Victoria and Corina watching Friedrich drive up the road on the tractor pulling the trailer full of apples they had just picked in the orchard, then unloading the apples in front of this building, and then sorting the apples, those for market, those to store, and those for making cider, which they carry inside. I can imagine them bringing in the grapes they had picked, and pressing them, and storing the juice in a barrel until it was ready to bottle. And here they brought in the eggs they had collected, the apricots, the peaches, the plums, the pears, and berries, too, and perhaps the vegetables from the garden. On these worn worktables they sorted and packaged and bottled. In this quaint white icebox they had chunks of ice to cool what needed cooling. All the farm life went through this building, this room and the feed room and fowl pens next door. And now I was dealing with the leavings.

TODAY THE horses wait for me in the orchard by the fence I built to keep them off the bank of the lower ditch. When they see me coming, see me slip around the gatepost, they cross the bridge, walk through the barn, and come up into the narrow corral at the foot of the main ditch. They stand there, looking, waiting. I reach out to the old one. He suffers one touch, then backs off. The younger one, the buckaroo, Gayle's horse, is more tractable. But he, too, is impatient. It is not for petting they came, or to pass the rest of the morning. It is to let me know that it is late, once more it is late. They have not been fed yet. When are they going to be fed?

This is winter talk. In summer and fall they can feed themselves on orchard grass. In spring, too. But this is still February.

Melting-snow time, mud time, freezing-nights time. The grasses are gone. What remains is brown. Inedible, they say. And if I do not feed them soon, they will start back on tree bark, right? Apple-tree bark.

I slide the loop off the top of the two-by-two gate frame, step into the orchard, refasten the wire, climb over the low wooden border, open the gate, and measure half a bale of timothy with my arms. I turn to carry it over the ditch, and the horses are standing there, blocking the way. All right, all right! I push the old one and drop the hay in two even helpings. Now it is time for winter watering; I remove from the horse barrel the big round of ice frozen over night and lean it against the fence next to the un-melted disks of ice from previous nights. I am careful not to break the ice disks; I like to look at these rough crystals all lined up. Now I go into the shed and fill a five-gallon bucket with water and carry it back to the barrel and pour it in. Thus I refill the horse barrel bucketful by bucketful until spring when I can take out the hose again.

I WAKE up in the dark. Did I hear the geese? Or was it dogs, or coyotes? Or some voice coming out of the walls or the vigas and latillas or the foot and a half of earth on top of them? Gayle sleeps beside me. We sleep in the room where Father Meyers slept, where he read his books and his mail, composed his homi-lies, wrote his letters, and died. He has been gone longer than he lived here, yet I feel his prayers, his curses, his repentings, his supplications, his hopes, and his despair seeping through these three-foot walls like snowmelt from the hill.

I sense women's voices, too: Victoria, Father Meyers's compan-ion, friend, devotee, perhaps his cousin, perhaps his paramour, as some say, and mother of his child, if there was a child; Corina, keeper of the house, the secrets, the memories, preserver and survivor; and Annelise, who taught and crocheted. Maybe others. The voice of Leona Bickford who lived here in the twenties, in the one-room house whose roof, like ours, never stopped leaking.

And the voices of whomever lived here before that, when the acequia was dug two hundred years ago, and those who camped here and hunted here before that, at least back to the Anasazi hunter who left that round basalt spear point for Rick to find four thousand years later on the hill above this house. Perhaps that hunter stopped right here to call down to companions by the river, "We have a deer!"

But now I am imagining things; I am just a tired man awake in the middle of the night. Across the room from our bed stood the single bed Father Meyers slept in the last twenty years of his life. Over the bed hung his creed stitched in red letters on a white cloth: *Erwachet froh jeder Morgen*, Wake up joyful every morning! All right, I am awake, Lord. But I am not sure what you mean about joyful. Is it the joy of being alive? Or is it the joy of anticipating everlasting life?

ON MARCH 11, 1936, at San Ysidro Church, the Reverend Friedrich Meyers celebrated the twenty-fifth anniversary of his ordination. Born and ordained in Germany, he came to Santa Fe in 1912 and served the archdiocese in the mountain villages in the north—Truchas, Las Trampas, Peñasco, Chamisal, Picuris Pueblo, Velarde, and Rio Oscuro. He supervised construction of the new church in Rio Oscuro, la Iglesia de San Ysidro, where his name was chiseled onto the cornerstone: Father Friedrich Meyers, 1929.

The card I hold now has gone soft with time, assumed that creamy yellow patina of age. It was printed for the occasion marking the taking of a vow—a promise that, unbeknownst to a nervous young cleric—held in its belly the seeds of an apple orchard in a dry country an ocean away:

"What think you? If a man have an hundred sheep, and one of them should go astray: does he not leave the ninety-nine in the mountains, and go to seek that which is gone astray?" Matthew: 18,12

Remembrance of the

SILVER SACERDOTAL JUBILEE

of

REV. FRIEDRICH MEYERS

Born June 25, 1885 in
Kuckhoven, Rheinland, Germany
Ordained March 11, 1911 in Cologne Cathedral
for the Archdiocese of Santa Fe, New Mexico.
First Solemn Mass March 19, 1911
in Kuckhoven, Rheinland, Germany
Twenty-fifth Anniversary
Rio Oscuro, New Mexico March 11, 1936

PRAY FOR ME

In October 1941 Father Meyers received this mimeographed letter from the Archdiocese of Santa Fe:

Dear Reverend Father:

No doubt, you have been aware of the fact that the Defense Program of our country includes a campaign for the sale of Defense Bonds and Stamps.

I have been requested to have the Priests make an announcement from the pulpit urging their people to do their part. I feel that this is not an unreasonable request and that every Priest should be glad to tell his people about it. . . .

No other document we have found here connects Father Meyers with the war against his native Germany. An entry in his diary for June 7, 1944, D day plus one, looks like a note to say a prayer for the success of the invasion: "Misa—cunturie—Invasion." But I could be misreading it. At the bottom of the same page he recorded, "2 trips to Rio Oscuro. Trip to Española. groceries—$2.80 car repaired—$9.00."

On June 22, 1944, Father Meyers wrote to the archdiocese:

His Excellency
The Most Rev. Archbishop
E. V. Byrne
Santa Fe N.M.

Most Rev. and Dear Archbishop,

I am very sorry to inform your Excellency that I feel un-
able to take care of Rio Oscuro parish. I was and I am willing
to do all I can, but I feel that I can not go any further.

For this coming Sunday I have announced the first mass at
nine in Vallecita and the second mass at eleven in Rio Oscuro.
From the way I am now, I am not able to be there and therefore I beg your Excellency to have another priest here already
for this coming Sunday. . . .

Under what circumstances he sent that letter I do not know.
He left the ministry officially sometime after World War II. It
was then that he built his private chapel onto the west end of this
farmhouse and cut a doorway to it through the three-foot-thick
stone wall of his study, which was also his sleeping room. He said
his last mass in this chapel in 1957. And here his body was laid
out for the rosary.

We know very little about Annelise Schaffle. She was from
Germany; letters told us that. She did fine needlework; we found
many examples in an outbuilding. She was also petite; the shoes
and dresses were tiny. Was she a nun? Was she a relative of
Meyers? Did she work for the school, or the church?

Victoria Howser, according to what old-timers have told us,
was a woman to be reckoned with right up to the end of her life
at ninety-three. There was nothing on the farm Howser could
not do. She drove the tractor, ran the rototiller, planted, cultivated, and harvested. She drove her '48 Dodge stake-bed truck
around the village selling what people did not come to the farm
to buy. She and Corina put up thousands of quarts of fruits and
vegetables. She must have helped make some of those gallons

upon gallons of wine left behind and become vinegar by the time we arrived. And she left a legacy of blossoms and flowers.

She left roses: red, deep red, pink, yellow, white, and the copper Austrian briar. She bordered the road with bridal wreath, snowball, honeysuckle, flowering quince, and many, many others whose names I do not know. She naturalized day lilies and sweet peas. Spring and summer and fall there was always something in bloom, in the orchard, the vineyard, along the drive, or in front of the house. Victoria also brought the memory of her native Pennsylvania in the vines and flowers painted on the white wooden front of the stone barn. Besides her plantings and regardless of her personal relationship or kinship to Friedrich Meyers (or less than kin and more than kind), Victoria's life is embedded in this farm in the childhood memories of her survivors, nephew Harry Howser, whom we met when he revisited the farm, and his children. Their names appear along with Corina's name as beneficiaries of the proceeds from the sale of the farm to us: Corina Coronado, 40 percent; Mrs. Patricia Rourke, 10 percent; Harry, 10 percent; Col. Joseph Howser, 10 percent; and Susan and Cathy Howser, 5 percent each. The story behind the remaining name, Mrs. Marion Rauscher, 20 percent, was cleared up only recently by one of our neighbors.

When Friedrich Meyers died, Victoria did not have the money to bury him. Marion Rauscher, a family friend, wanted to pay for the funeral, but his wife insisted it be a loan for which she wanted collateral. The only thing Victoria had was the farm, and thus the Rauschers acquired the 20 percent. Rauscher did not like the arrangement, I was told, and he intended to tear up the promissory note, but he died without doing so. Mrs. Rauscher was more than happy to collect on the debt when Victoria died and we bought the farm.

Perhaps the voices I think I hear tonight belong to the orchard; some of its trees are probably older than we are. The orchard passed itself on to us—that's what it feels like—because we were willing to become its caretakers. We have tried to do the

right thing by the orchard, to the best of our knowledge and be-
liefs. And we are no different from countless others who have
cared for orchards in their times; we have learned by doing and
observing. We are learning still.

AMONG THE papers left behind by Father Meyers and Victoria
Howser was a 1946 "Professional Growers" edition of the Stark
Brothers Nursery fruit-tree catalog. It must have been one of
their early color catalogs because the reproduction of apple and
peach and plum photographs was fuzzy and not true-toned. This
was before the era of high-speed, low-cost, high-quality color reproduction. I remember particularly the Elephant Heart Plum
offering, not so much because of the photograph, which barely
resembles the red-fleshed Elephant Hearts we grow, but because
of the information about the origin of this plum. It came from
the hand of the American plant breeder who developed the nectarine and the Shasta daisy, Luther Burbank. The copy boasted
that it was Stark Brothers Nursery that Burbank chose to carry
on his work and offer to the world his plum, his nectarine, and
other creations.

I think Father Meyers and Victoria used that catalog to order
apple trees. Next to the list of apple trees offered that year I noticed several check marks. Many times have I wished I could go
over the list, look up the descriptions of the marked varieties, and
then take those descriptions into the orchard and compare with
the fruit of our questionable and unknown varieties. But several
years ago I loaned the catalog to a man who was planting an orchard of heirloom apple trees. I saw him later and asked about
the catalog; he was surprised that I should ask because, he said,
he had photocopied the catalog and mailed back the original.

The apple has been in the patrimony of the human race
longer than any written historical record we have. We can trace
the origin of the apple to western Asia, and we have evidence of
its wide cultivation by prehistoric peoples. The apple is as close to
being a universal fruit as any we have. Perhaps that's what makes
it a good choice for the object lesson in the Garden of Eden. And

wherever apples are grown today, which is in every land of temperate climate, people spend their lives searching for new varieties, preserving and recovering authentic old varieties, and trying out new ways to grow the ones they have.

Stark Brothers announced in a recent mailing that cuttings from a bona fide Johnny Appleseed tree found in Nova, Ohio, in 1994 had been propagated at the nursery and now four- to five-foot trees could be purchased from them, each with a "Certificate of Authenticity." The apple is green and tart, good for baking, sauce, and eating fresh, and is what Chapman called a Rambo apple. Since John Chapman—the given name of the legendary seeder—died in 1845, the tree in Ohio has to be more than 150 years old to be authentic, and the photograph in the catalog bears that out. The trunk is large and gnarled. It is open in the middle, and there are holes where its two main branches used to be. Now just two small branches come off to the left and one small one to the right. This ancient one, green and still alive, sitting now in front of a white suburban-looking house in a manicured lawn with flowers and shrubs around it, is reportedly the last survivor of John Chapman's noble enterprise of sowing apple trees wherever he wandered in the pioneer West.

Thirty years ago the United States Department of Agriculture's Plant Introduction Station in Glenn Dale, Maryland, had more than 800 varieties of named and unnamed apples under cultivation. Each tree had a number and a history. Size, shape, color, flesh, and flavor of fruit from each year's harvest was recorded along with notations on quality and harvest date. Horticulturist William Ackerman studied 58 varieties to find new stock resistant to late-spring frosts. I like the names and descriptions of his subjects. Winter Queening, a crimson-striped, aromatic fruit also known as Old English Pearmain, went back to Norfolk in the year 1200, 187 years before Chaucer's first Canterbury Tale. In 1995 Southmeadow Fruit Gardens listed six Pearmains among its choice 152 varieties of apples: Adams, Blue, Claygate, Lamb Abbey, Summer, and White Winter. Adams Pearmain took its name from the man who brought it to the London

Horticultural Society in 1826. It was known as Hanging Pearmain in Hertfordshire where it came from. Winter Queening, the possible mother of all Pearmains, blossomed April 30th in Ackerman's study, which was eight days later than Yellow Delicious but fourteen days earlier than a French cider apple named Bedan.

Bedan, also known as Bec d'Angle and Petit doux de Bretagne, was traced back to 1363. Its flesh was "creamy, crisp, juicy, and sweet"; on my tongue its names are just as delectable, especially Petit doux de Bretagne, Little Sweet One from Brittany. Somehow Bedan never made it to Southmeadow, or if it did, it was under another name. Because of its late blossoming date, May 14th, Bedan would have an excellent chance of escaping late-spring frost damage if grown in Rio Oscuro; nobody here ever remembers a killing frost after May 15th.

Other names from Ackerman's 58 ring appealingly in my ear: Binet Violet, also from France; Gewürzluiken from Germany; Flaskeeple from Norway; and Piekne Oltarzewa from Poland. I wonder about the fate of these good-named apple trees and the others of the 58 the horticulturist selected for his study of late-blossoming foreign apples. They had been growing for twenty years when the report was published in 1963, along with some 750 other named and unnamed varieties. Have any of the 58 been considered commercially marketable in this country? If they are still growing at Glenn Dale today, still being observed, harvested, and tasted, their histories still kept, someone must be pruning them sufficiently "to maintain tree vigor and to allow adequate spray coverage," one of the conditions of the study. I hope that one day one of Ackerman's successors at Glenn Dale will be funded to use some of these varieties in a nontoxic, biological growing program and will record how such a program affects the quality of fruit, and the quality of the soil, and the bird and insect life over the short-term and the long-term.

Clearly, once we take something out of nature, like a chicken, or a cow, or a fruit tree, we cannot abandon it to any natural process. It will need our help. The question is what kind of help.

Biological farming or natural farming is a relatively new concept, a reaction to the costs and long-range effects of modern maximum-yield farming. As defined by Masanobu Fukuoka in *The One-Straw Revolution,* natural farming means using the simplest techniques and working with and within the natural process, as opposed to using sophisticated machinery and complex techniques to reshape nature into a human-serving mold. The former is sustainable because it renews soil and does not depend upon high-cost inputs of nonrenewable resources. But farming naturally takes more than just desire. When he took over his father's citrus orchard, Fukuoka let two acres of mandarin oranges fend for themselves—no pruning, and nothing else. The branches grew into each other, insects attacked, and the trees all died. What then was the natural pattern for citrus trees in Japan? "In the process of arriving at the answer," he wrote, "I wiped out another 400 trees."

I do not know of anyone who is searching for natural patterns in apple trees. Perhaps there are no archetypal forms for each of the dozens of named and unnameable varieties of mature trees growing in this orchard at 5,900 feet in northern New Mexico. However, this is not a question of vital concern in our community. Trees are pruned for function: to produce large fruit, to be easy to pick, to be easy to spray. Even those orchard owners who do not prune, who let things go, do not disagree with the proper husbandmen; orchard care just doesn't fit into all lifestyles. We have no Fukuoka to suggest that each tree find its own path. To even hint that an apple tree or any other fruit tree might have an "own path" is an idea as foreign here as it was in Japan.

I try to imagine Saint Francis of Assisi reincarnated as a Rio Oscuro apple grower who now hears the Lord speaking from his trees as well as from birds and animals. San Francisco tells his neighbors they should "listen to the tree" before they attack with their pruning saws. Even if the devout believed Francisco was the genuine article, and his words were sacred, in matters of pruning they would probably adhere to the advice of the doctor of horticulture at our agricultural research station and the publications of our state university and the multitude of experts in the great apple-growing centers of our country.

Someday a cidermaster may write a chapter in his memoirs called "what the apple trees and I have learned from each other about pruning." He may say that his own attitude and practice were as important as anything he read in books or pamphlets. He may say that the commitment to openness in the beginner's mind had to be renewed and renewed each time he stood under a tree with his sharpened pruning shears. He may say he had no mute, no unimportant trees in his orchard, as the birder finds no unimportant birds, and the marriage partners no unimportant words.

FEBRUARY 13TH

The red dog crosses the straw-colored field. I call her, and we walk together down to the big orchard. The light snow has turned to rain. Patches of snow hold on in the shadows of the ditch bank and the barn, but the ground is thawing. We walk around mud ponds churned up by the horses, around the tangles of tree trimmings, around the low-hanging branches still to be trimmed. The trees stand quietly in the drizzle, leafless, birdless, feigning the gray-brown sleep of winter. Today I do not disturb them. I am looking for six particular trees to show to the tree pruners, Antonito and his father. And I am angry with myself.

In our first winter on the farm Antonito and his father appeared with a simple proposition. The orchard needed pruning. They were experienced tree pruners. They would prune six trees at four dollars a tree, to show us what they could do.

Gayle and I looked at them. Antonito was about twenty. He said they had pruned a lot of trees in Rio Oscuro. "You know Johnsons' orchard?" No, we didn't know them. "We pruned their trees, the whole orchard."

"I'm fifty years old," the older man said; "he's my son." The father turned and walked back to his truck. Antonito followed. They both spat.

Antonito came back. "We can go look. You pick the ones you want." We asked him to wait, and we walked up the hill.

We had little money to get through the winter. But the orchard had not been pruned for years, maybe decades. We didn't know anyone who pruned trees in the village; we'd been on the land just a few months. And four dollars seemed more than reasonable. "Do you think they know what they're doing?" Gayle said.

"I don't know. I think they've been drinking."

"Yes. But we've got to decide. It's only six trees."

"At least it's a start." We went down into the orchard with them to pick out the trees.

They walked ahead of us, talking to each other. They stopped by a tree four rows from the road. They spit. "This one?" Antonito said.

"No," Gayle said, "not so close to the road. Beyond the pump house," and she pointed.

"No?" Antonito looked puzzled.

"Beyond the pump house," she said again, and pointed again.

Finally we agreed on six trees. "Then if you like we can do them all?" Antonito said.

"Six trees," I said; "then we'll see."

Gayle went back to the house. They drove into the orchard to the first tree we had selected, and the father took out the chainsaw. The father started the saw, held it at full throttle, and attacked the tree. The chain spewed white chips. The great limb listed, then lurched, and toppled to the ground. I winced as it hit. Now Antonito climbed into the crotch of the tree. The father handed him the saw. A second limb fell. Then a third. Then the fourth. Now the tree looked like a man with four stumped arms reaching to heaven. Antonito handed back the saw.

The father turned it off, put it down. They both went back to the truck. I left. As I climbed the bank I looked back. They were walking away from the truck, spitting.

It took me days to clean up, cut the heavy limbs and the

smaller branches, load the van, drive up to the house, separate the pieces to be split from the pieces to be stacked. One of the trees barely leafed out the next summer; the following year it was gone. Another lasted two more years. The shock from cutting off the major limbs of these mature trees was more than they could stand. Perhaps 80 percent of their branches and twigs, the structures that carried the nascent buds and leaves for the next year, were gone. It was too much. Others found ways to survive, though it would be years before they recovered. Every time I walked by those trees I felt sick, as though we had betrayed something. And we had. We had thought those men knew what they were doing; they had told us so. And I believed them. Shame on me.

Antonito reappeared last fall, dead sober, his wife beside him, his pickup filled with wood. "Pine. And piñon." He forced out the words, one at a time, as though trying to speak when he was sober took a great effort. "Split. Dry." His eye twitched. The red razor nick on his cheek quivered.

It looked all right, I said. A hundred dollars, he said. I shook my head. We cut our own. For a moment he said nothing. His wife said something in Spanish. Then, maybe I knew someone else who might want some wood, some good wood?

Our neighbors also cut their own. Well, maybe someone. Maybe I could tell someone he had wood, good wood.

I wish I had left it at that. I wish that at that moment I had called up my anger at the mess he had made of those trees. And just let him go. Let-him-go—that's what I thought. But he was trying so hard to be sober. So I said maybe, maybe later in the winter, in February, he might come back and we might have some trees to prune.

A week ago he did come back to see about pruning, and I told him right off that this time we would set up conditions. First off no sauce on the job. He agreed. He said they would like to work under a contract, for the whole orchard, all the trees that needed pruning. No way—I said we would commit to six trees only. And we will look at each tree I select and discuss how it should be cut.

Only after we see what they do on the first will they start on the others. I told him to come back the next week and I would have the trees marked and he could tell me what it would cost.

But this was not the way to hire a man to prune trees. And I knew it.

Today what I have in mind first are some tall trees that bear large red apples that seem to take a second growth after the late-season rains. Often they split open before we get to pick them. A neighbor told me they were old-fashioned Romes, and that's what I call them. They lack the bright color of the regular Red Romes, but they release almost the same perfume at first bite as the others.

The Rome does not have the tartness of a Jonathan or Wine-sap, or the full flavor of a Stayman. Nor does it make the mouth tingle as does the McIntosh. Yet we prize our Romes; these are the apples that give our cider that subtle, aromatic essence that reaches the olfactory sense just as the juice touches the lips.

We pass the barn and reach the first and largest of the old-fashioned Rome trees. The big Dane and the small terrier run toward us. The Dane barks as he always does when something excites him, even if it is only finding us walking in the orchard. I stop at the tree, and the three dogs run off toward the river. Halfway to the fence they turn and go after a rabbit as fast as they can. I call but do not expect them to hear me. And they don't. Now they chase magpies, now they chase each other.

I feel a little jealous. They are so excited. They spend so much energy. Like tennis players charging the net, skiers racing the slope.

The rain has stopped, but the brown ribs and tendrils above me are slow to release their drips, their drops. I admire this old tree, spreading into the misty sky, upwardly immobile. It is fixed, steady, heedless of what I or anyone else down here might think. It has grown into a great umbrella over the earth. Its lowest branches are at least seven feet off the ground; the tops of the crown are a good twenty feet and higher. Even with our tallest ladders, there is always higher fruit we cannot reach by hand.

Here the dense canopy of old and new branches, old and new shoots, also makes it difficult to maneuver a pole picker from the top of a ladder. For the picker's sake the tree should be thinned and topped.

I tie a red ribbon on the tall Rome. In this row are four others that have grown to the same size. I mark them, too. That leaves one. A few rows down there is one of the trees Antonito and his father attacked that first day. It is a Red Delicious. Over the years it has grown into a one-tree jungle. When I look at it now I feel a certain madness. I feel almost violent. I want to get even, somehow. I want them to fix this tree, them, nobody else.

Antonito is waiting for me when I come up the road. I lead him down into the orchard and show him the trees I have picked. He points to some small trees; what about those? I tell him I have marked the ones he will start with. And I ask how much they will cost. He says he will have to talk with his father; they will come over tomorrow.

They never come.

Man was made for Joy & Woe;
And when this we rightly know,
Through the World we safely go.
Joy & Woe are woven fine,
A Clothing for the Soul divine.
Under every grief & pine
Runs a joy with silken twine . . .
Throughout all these Human Lands
Tools were made, & Born were hands,
Every Farmer understands . . .
—William Blake

Nowhere in our purchase agreement is there anything about a covenant with the founders of these orchards. These trees in this lower orchard—mature, old, and very old—have become ours, unconditionally. And the apples and the pears, plums, peaches, apricots, nectarine, almond, English walnut in the orchards above. And the grapes and berries and mulberries without end—all this is here to do with as we please, as we feel is right.

I am not completely happy with the way the business with Antonito and his father ended. But even if he were really interested in pruning as opposed to savaging trees, his father was not. Yet now, as I walk along the row of giant Romes running eastward from the barn, the idea of unconditional ownership makes me uneasy. I turn to go between the rows of Double Red Delicious along the fence and stop at the biggest regular Red Delicious, where the upper fence intersects along the main lateral. The good, heavy limbs reach over the fences and over the ditch like a living sculpture pointing out the sacred mountains and the four directions. Who am I or who is any man or woman that this tree should be mindful of one of us?

I run my hand over the westerly limb. The skin is smooth, young, for all the tree's fifty years. I check the pulse. The tree lives, winter or not. Its intentions are clear: to wait out the winter, to blossom out in the spring, to absorb water from this ditch all summer, to ripen its fruit in the fall, to fight off the enemies that worm and crawl and fly, to welcome the bees and wasps, to endure the ladders and the pickers, and then to give in to winter next, and wait again for spring.

I pass rows of McIntosh running north from the pump house, then turn west to the Yellow Transparents, our earliest cider apples; their rows run south to the rusting hay rake and the wooden stock trailer against the fence, heaped with bleached and broken fruit boxes. And I circle back to las Manzanas de Julio, which ripen even earlier than the Transparents, racing those bright-red tart apples in the far-east corner by the river to be the very first apples in our valley.

I consider all of these and the other varieties I can name and more whose names I do not know, all Victoria and Friedrich and their people planted here. Trees, vineyards, terraces. Thousands of feet of hand-dug irrigation ditches. Dozens and dozens of concrete gates, many now slumping into the ground but at one time new, hand-mixed concrete poured into measured, fitted wooden forms. And the outbuildings, those still standing and in use, those already collapsed by time. Everywhere is their imprint, from the shrine of Our Lady of the Orchard above the acequia to the old, now broken line of Lombardy poplars reaching heavenward, a row of living watchtowers for birds and angels guarding the orchard and the road.

Finally I stop by an ancient-looking Stayman, bark-bald over half its limbs and much of the rest pocked by sapsuckers and woodpeckers gleaning borers and the like. It has less than a third of its cambium intact. And yet its branches live, have the tiny swellings that turn into blossoms and, if all goes well, into fruit.

The best fruit I have ever tasted has come from this orchard. It has come from ancient trees, trees that long ago made their treaties with this soil, this water, this complex of bacteria and insects and birds, the air currents flowing down from the mesa through the narrow passages of canyons and arroyos, across the orchard to the river, the moisture, the sounds of the river day and river night, and the sounds, hands, and tools of las Obscuranas. That the treaties have been kept and have worked is proved in the fruit.

Walking back through the orchard I think of the covenant that is not and the treaties we had nothing to do with. I do not feel these trees belong to us. I serve them as much as they serve me. As we are adapting, so are they. As we are learning how to live cheek-and-jowl with people in an ever more crowded world, learning how to breathe pollutants, accept radiation, eat additives and impurities, so are the trees adapting to global warming and the extreme cold and extreme heat pursuant thereto. So are the coyotes chasing the rabbit adapting. And the birds that eat the worms and larvae that would eat our fruit work. All of us are changing, and where we will end, no one can foretell.

As I encounter change in every facet of life I feel more and more a part of the pruning process, pruning and at the same time being pruned. I clip a water sprout, I cut away a false direction in my life. And all those dead branches Gayle and I and Olaf cut away in this orchard thirteen years ago felt like lifting so much of the deadwood I had been carrying for decades. We lifted burdens from the trees so they could get on with their lives and we with ours. What a joy to haul out that dead apple wood, saw it up, and burn it in the old Ashley to keep us warm through the first winters. Progress!

When we were new on this land a man from down the road came by with his wife to meet us. Sometime during the conversation he stopped and shook his head. "It's too bad that you have such a miserable-looking orchard," he said. "Your place could really be nice, but I don't envy you the work."

"What do you mean?" I asked.

"Look at those wild trees. It will take years to make your trees as neat and trim as ours." He shook his head again.

I said nothing. I had seen his orchard. The trees were all short and well groomed, and apparently all the same age. I had seen many orchards like that. Pruned, sprayed, the grass mowed short. They did look like the work of good caretakers. Yet those were not my kind of orchards.

Pruning Tools
Lopping shears and anvil shears
Hand clippers and hand loppers
Pruning saws—folding ones, straight ones with sheaths
Bow saws
A 20-inch, lightweight Homelite chainsaw

Besides the standard pruning tools we have a special bonsai pruning tool introduced to us by Brad Park, a friend from Santa Fe who is interested in permaculture. The tool looks like the pliers a farrier uses to pull out nails from horseshoes, except that the head is offset for pruning. Brad demonstrated the tool on a small branch. "See how it makes a hollow cut?" He pointed to the upraised edges. "The life of a tree is here in the cambium; the smallest piece of cambium can sustain life, and without it there is no life. Healing takes place as the cambium collar grows down over the hollow center. That's the advantage over the proud cut of the saw blade or a standard pruning shears."

He showed us how the bonsai tool was also good for trimming bark around a wound, for cleaning out wood in the crotch of a tree, and cleaning the wound in an old pruning cut to keep out moisture and bugs.

Pruning Notes

The branch system of a tree matches its root system; you cut branches, you kill roots. (Brad) And vice versa.

Fruit trees are not really trees; more like fruit bushes. They may grow into each other and strangle themselves. (Brad and Fukuoka)

When you understand pruning through and through, you understand everything. When you try to understand all there is to know, you understand nothing. (after Shunryo Suzuki)

The help we need will arrive when we are ready. But it will never be what we expect. *(The Cidermaster's Handbook)*

BOSQUE DEL Apache Wildlife Refuge on the Rio Grande about a hundred miles south of Albuquerque is winter home to tens of thousands of snow geese, Canada geese, and sandhill cranes. I like Bosque del Apache best on late afternoons around the beginning of the year when the sky fills with wings as the geese and cranes return to their ponds of the night. I like to stop just at dark, get out of the car, listen. Ten thousand, maybe a hundred thousand birds calling. It sounds like the creation of the earth. I have heard this a dozen times, and the wonder never diminishes. Then the ranger finishes her evening sweep, finds the stragglers listening and watching there, and sends everybody home.

Toward the end of January birds begin heading north. As the days grow longer I hear them over the farm, great vees honking their way up the Rio Grande. I want to call out, to wish them good flight, safe flight. I want to let them know I'll be looking for them next year down at Bosque. But it's not necessary. They know all that they want to know.

Often as not, as spring approaches, other migrants also come our way. Sometimes they carry rucksacks and walk up the drive. Sometimes they come in the cars of neighbors who have found them hitchhiking or at their own doorsteps in the village. They have come from Alsace, Israel, the northern coast of Washington, Chihuahua, Minnesota, Iowa. They also come from nearby, Albuquerque, Santa Fe, Española, Taos.

"Do you have work?"

"Yes. The orchard needs pruning. Fences need mending, ditches need digging. But we do not have much money."

For the most part they are willing to do anything we suggest in return for a place to stay and something to eat. But rarely do they know anything about farmwork. Some have stayed a few days, some a couple of weeks; some decide not to stay.

Robert and Germaine, two young men from France just finished with their military service, were seeing America. They were on their way to work and vacation in the Northwest when a neighbor picked them up on the Taos highway. He told them there was plenty of work in Rio Oscuro, and so for a couple of weeks they were passed from farm to farm. For us they dug a trench for a drain, and they picked apricots. In the evenings they talked about their hometown in Alsace and their work, Robert as salesman, Germaine as pastry chef. We spoke in German, a little English, a little French. In between they chattered in a most musical tongue that I had never heard before, Alsatian. On their last evening Germaine made us a tart with apricots they had picked. I watched him blend the flour and butter, roll the dough, form it, and bake it. I watched him set the perfectly cut pieces of fruit in the custard. This was an artist at work. My hands could not do anything like that in this lifetime. And Germaine's tart tasted as good as it looked. Robert left us the address of his parents. If we ever get to Alsace, I would like to look up these men, see what if anything from America rubbed off on them and their families.

Tim, from Iowa, was passed on to us by neighbors who ran out of work for him and ran out of patience with his ways. Tim did have farming experience, but he knew nothing about northern New Mexico. We wanted a four-wire horse fence along the drive. For three days he pounded the posthole digger into the ground, working without a shirt or hat in the strong New Mexico sun. On the fourth day he was sick with sunstroke.

At the supper table the second night he wanted to read us Gerard Manley Hopkins, his favorite poet. We said okay. He put down his fork and picked up his book and began in a loud monotone:

> How to keep—is there any, is there none such, nowhere known some bow or brooch or braid or brace, lace, latch or catch or key to keep
> Back beauty, keep it, beauty, beauty, beauty, . . . from vanishing away?
> O, is there no frowning of these wrinkles, ranked wrinkles deep,
> Down? . . .

"Wait a minute," Gayle said. "What does that mean to you?"

He looked at her. "It doesn't mean anything. I just like the sound."

"Oh. Well, maybe it would be better if we just ate quietly tonight?"

But the next night he was back with *Moby Dick*, reciting his favorite passages from memory. Finally Gayle told him, gently, that she was a visual person, she liked to read to herself, and she didn't really enjoy being read to. Then he talked, about his sister who was running for Congress and how he had helped her. He talked about a girlfriend he had had in California. And about his stay in the hospital in Washington. In everything he said there was a feeling of the impersonal, as though he were talking of abstract things that did not affect him. He talked to us as if to an impersonal audience, not two people he was having a conversation with over dinner. And every few days he would say, "I need a break. I need to go into the mountains to camp. I need to be alone."

"That's fine," we would say. "Just let us know in advance so we won't be counting on you."

Tim did good work. We planned a trip and asked if we could leave him in charge. Sure, he said, and was there anything special we would like him to do? We said he might prune the grapes. He might clear the thornbushes and wild roses from the path down from the acequia to the pole barn. He said he would do it, and we left. We were gone about two weeks. When we came back he showed us what he had done. He had cleared all vegetation from the path, and he had cut down a cottonwood we were nurturing as a shade tree, the only one growing that far up the hill. Then at the end of the path he had cut all the bottom branches from a perfectly cone-shaped juniper that had delighted us every time we passed it. Up on the acequia he had not only cut all the willows and wild roses, which we wanted him to do, but he cut everything else, including the trees shading the bank all the way from the water gate at the top of the path to the house. And at the end of the three main rows of grapes he had cut off all the branches from a good apricot, because they were shading the grapes.

We were speechless. We went inside to recover. "We can't trust him to do anything on his own," I said.

"We have to talk with him," Gayle said.

Tim was a problem for me. I was not a good manager. For the most part I wanted to show someone the job, give him the tools, and then let him do his work while I went off and did mine. Pruning, picking fruit, cleaning ditches—I wanted to be able to let the worker do the jobs at hand as if it were his own place and he was working in the best possible way for the best result. Yes, on some things we would work together, but not all or most things. And I wanted the helper to get out and get the job going without me being there. I had lots of things to do and think about on the farm and in my life. Being a role model for a helper was a very low priority for me.

At lunch Gayle thanked Tim for taking good care of the house, watering the plants, and feeding the animals. After lunch we took another walk with him along the acequia. "We appreciate all the work you have done," Gayle said. "But you have to understand that the look of things is also very important to me, probably more important than anything else. I liked the trees hanging over the ditch. Now it looks bare, ugly. Next time before you cut any trees or branches up where I look at them, please ask me."

Tim looked at her blankly, and said nothing.

"You did a good job on the path," I said. "But you could have gone around the cottonwood and the juniper on the slope. They stabilize the soil, hold the earth in place when we have the downpours." He looked at me, again without saying anything. "But I guess it's my fault; I never told you exactly what I wanted."

At supper that night Tim seemed jumpy. "I have to get away," he said. "I really want to go camping up in the mountains. I want to be alone. I need to meditate."

"Can you wait until after the New Mexico Arts and Crafts show?" Gayle asked. "We need someone to take care of the animals while we're in Albuquerque."

"I don't know," Tim said.

"It's in two weeks," Gayle said. "Or if you do go camping now, can you be back in time to stay here?"

He thought for a minute. "I guess I'll wait," he said. Two days later, early in the morning before we got up, Tim left. There was no note. Most of his books and half his clothes and his boots and other gear were still in his room. And he never called, he never wrote, he never came back. Finally we shipped his things to his father in Iowa.

Although Tim's departure was inconvenient, it was a relief to have the house, the farm, and the dinner table, especially the table, to ourselves again. A half-year later Tim wrote a postcard to the neighbor whom he had stayed with before coming to us.

He was living in a religious community, he wrote, and was "taking care of his soul." The card ended with a question: "Have you come to find the Lord in your heart?" The neighbor wrote back that his relationship with God was his own private business. Tim has never written to us. I would like to hear from him, but I don't know what I would answer if he did write. I could tell him that his fence posts are just as solid as when he packed them in.

IN THE last row at the east end of the orchard there is one tall, well-proportioned Double Red Delicious tree that I associate with a small man in his thirties whom I hoped would be a big help in our orchard. It was also in February that he appeared first. I remember this man standing in the crotch of that tree, his black city shoes braced against the limbs, his arms reaching up with the aluminum-handled lopping shears, the solid, sharp ones that made him smile when I handed them to him. He looks, he snips a branch, reaches higher, snips another, looks again, snips once more, and moves to a new footing. Through my own eyes I see the image he has in his of the finished tree and how he will trim to achieve that image.

In the corner of my mind just beyond the trees I see two women. I remember the hope in their faces when each was with him.

The first woman lived in our village. She had befriended this man, and given him a place to stay. Then she brought him to the farm to help him find work. The woman was perhaps in her late thirties or early forties, heavy, but with a warm, sincere look that I have seen many times in women from northern New Mexico. I thought I had seen her before in the general store in the village. She introduced us. Jesus Bonda said he had grown up in the apple orchards of Chihuahua. He knew pruning. He had left Mexico when he was fifteen. He had worked in Santa Fe, but now he wanted to get out in the country. He needed work, for whatever we could pay. All this he told us in good English, which he had taught himself. We hired him.

The next morning we walked down to the orchard. It was a little muddy and he was wearing polished city shoes, but that was his business. We walked to the east fence. We looked at two large Red Delicious, a large Winesap, an early McIntosh, all in the last row next to the fence. We talked about topping so we could pick the topmost fruit from the twelve-foot orchard ladder. We talked about opening the centers so the fruit would get more sun and the pickers could more easily reach the fruit. We talked about taking only one branch in five, leaving enough surface so the tree would not go into shock.

"What about these other trees?"

"They need pruning too. But do these first."

"Okay."

"I'll come back to see how you're doing."

He smiled. "Okay."

I started to leave, then stopped. "Did you bring a lunch?"

"No."

"All right, I'll make you a sandwich. And bring down water. Tomorrow you can bring a lunch."

"Okay."

By lunchtime he had finished the two large Red Delicious in the corner and was about to start the Winesap. We walked around his work together. If the trees had mirrors to look at themselves, they would have been pleased. All the tangle was gone. Each limb stood free, supporting its own branches, reaching up freely, without interference. For me that much cutting would have taken a whole day, at least. And he had missed nothing.

He looked at me. "Is that what you wanted?"

"They look good, Jesus."

He smiled. "Okay. But I don't like to be called Jesus. I'm not that holy. Just call me Jesse."

He worked the afternoon, the next day, and the day after. He finished sixteen trees. Then we ran out of money.

We talked, trying to figure out a way that he could do more work for us until summer when we started making something from the farm. Jesse said he was living in his friend's old adobe house next to her mobile home.

"She is a good person. She takes care of me. But the house has no heat. It is hard being cold at night and in the morning."

"Yes," I said. "We will try to think of something, and we will let you know."

Jesse needed a warm place to stay. We needed someone to work in the orchard, but we'd had enough of people staying in our house. Gayle and I talked about buying a small camping trailer for him to stay in. He could work for the rent and utilities. Maybe he could also work for neighbors to get money. And in the summer we could pay him something when we sold fruit and cider at the market.

I talked with Jesse on the phone, and he seemed to like the idea. We looked at inexpensive camping trailers in various states of repair. Finally we found one in Santa Fe, parked near the racetrack. When we got home, I went to find Jesse. The little adobe house was in a compound among a larger family house, a modern trailer home, and some other buildings. He came to the door, shook my hand, asked me in. His room was bright with Mexican blankets on a wall and on the bed, a table, some shelves with his clothes, some magazines, some books, a chair. There was no stove. "This is where I live." He nodded at the bed, the chair, the shelves. He smiled.

I told him about the trailer. He said he would try to borrow his friend's pickup to tow the trailer to the farm. Two days later Jesse drove up to the house with his friend in her big V-8 Chevy pickup, and we all three drove to Santa Fe to get the trailer. We attached the trailer to the ball hitch on the truck, but we could not figure out how to connect the trailer's taillights to the truck's light system. "Don't worry," Jesse said; "it will be all right. I used to drive big trucks for a living." He smiled at the woman, and she smiled back at him.

Jesse drove carefully through Santa Fe and stayed below forty-five on the highway. I was concerned that we might be stopped because of the trailer's license plate, which was thirty years out of date. I also suspected that Jesse did not have a New Mexico driver's license. But we made it to the farm, and Jesse backed the trailer into the place I had cleared for it next to the garden.

The trailer had not been lived in for some time, and it took Gayle and me a week to clean it. I hooked up a water line and discovered leaks in the copper tubing that I had to fix. I also had to put in a new toilet. When it seemed livable I called Jesse's friend and asked her to have Jesse call us. A week passed; he did not call or appear. I called again. He came over the next evening. He sat down on the couch, made himself comfortable, smiled, and then he told us a story about having lived in a large trailer in Santa Fe, much more comfortable than ours, and rent free, just for taking care of some property.

"Now I'm living in my friend's little house for nothing. She cooks for me. She bought me a suit so we could go to her church together. It does not seem wise for me to move into this little trailer and then have to work for staying there." He finished and he smiled.

There goes the help with pruning, I thought.

"Why didn't you tell us before?" Gayle asked. "We would not have spent money for the trailer if it were not for you."

"Maybe you have some money to pay me."

"No," I said, "not now."

He shrugged apologetically. He had come to see us and had explained his situation; what more could he do? He left. As far as we were concerned, that was the end of Jesse for us.

THAT WAS in March. In June Jesse reappeared, this time with another woman. She was Anglo, in her forties, dressed like a woman who spent a lot of time outdoors. She said she raised horses down in the valley and Jesse was staying with her, helping her out.

Jesse spoke up. "Do you have work?"

"We have no money," I said.

The woman went up to the house with Gayle to look at paintings.

Jesse lit a cigarette and offered me one. I shook my head. He pulled a half-pint of whiskey from his pocket. "Want a drink?"

"No, thanks."

He seemed agitated. This was a different Jesse from the calm, self-assured tree pruner I remembered. He pulled a small pipe from another pocket. "You want to smoke?"

"No, thanks."

"You sure you have no work? Maybe I can do some work and you pay me later?"

"No, I don't want to do that."

"I do good work."

"I know that. Look, when we have some money to pay you, I'll call you."

They left. Weeks later we read in the valley newspaper about a high-speed auto chase in a stolen car that landed two Mexican nationals in the county jail. One was named Jesus Bonda. Then we heard the story in other versions: the woman's car wasn't really stolen, just borrowed without permission; the driver wasn't Jesse, it was his brother; they weren't really drunk; they weren't really going a hundred miles an hour. Then Jesse called us.

The operator said we had a collect call from Jesus Bonda, would we accept the charges? I said yes.

"Harvey, it's Jesse."

There was a lot of noise in the background. "Where are you?"

"I'm in jail."

"Where?"

"In Santa Fe. Listen, can you tell my friend in the village? Tell her where I am. Tell her I want to see her."

"Can't you call her?"

"No. She doesn't have a phone. You have to tell her."

"Okay."

As I drove to the woman's house I guessed what her response would be. She had befriended Jesse, cooked for him, bought him a suit so he could go to church with her. Why he left, why he took up with someone else I didn't know. He had told me that he didn't drink, but that his brother had an alcohol problem. Yet he had a bottle when he came to the house. I did not want to bother this woman. I was sorry I offered. But Jesse needed help.

I drove into the compound. The little adobe Jesse had stayed in now looked abandoned. I went up to her trailer, which was next door. I knocked. She opened the door, looked at me, but said nothing.

"Jesse Bonda called me," I said. "He asked me to tell you where he is."

She looked sad. "I already know."

"He asked if you would go to see him."

"Thank you, but I never want to see him again."

"I'm sorry," I said, "sorry I bothered you."

"It's all right. It's not your fault."

A FEW days later Jesse called a second time, and a second time I accepted the charge. He asked if I went to see the woman. I said yes, and she didn't want to see him.

"I need a thousand dollars. That will fix everything. Can you get me a thousand dollars?"

"We don't have a thousand dollars."

"I'll work for you. I'll take care of you."

"We don't have a thousand dollars."

"I need a thousand dollars to get out." He sounded desperate.

"Look, I'll call New Mexico Legal Services. They might be able to help you. That's all I can do."

"Okay."

I called Legal Services and learned that they didn't take criminal cases and that Jesse would have a court-appointed attorney if he needed one.

Jesse called again. "Harvey, a thousand dollars will fix everything."

"How can that be? You still have to go to trial, maybe go to jail, maybe pay a fine."

"A thousand dollars will fix it," he said again.

"We don't have it," I said. "Please don't call anymore."

Months later Jesse made the front page of the *Santa Fe New Mexican*. Somehow he had been released from jail and was living with two other men in a trailer in Española. One night someone set that trailer on fire. Police called it a drug-related crime involving one of the other men. All three were asleep. All three burned to death, including Jesus Bonda, age thirty-four, from Chihuahua, Mexico.

Once, afterwards, I met the woman from our village who had introduced us to Jesse. She told me how bad she felt when he let her down. I could see it in her face. It was not anger. It was emptiness. I guess emptiness was my feeling, too. Jesse pruned apple trees as well as anyone I had seen, and better than most. He was a natural; he seemed to belong in an orchard.

THE VOLUNTEER pruners arrive one Saturday in February—six of them, flushed, enthusiastic, friends of our daughter Connie. We show them what they need. There are basic things to learn like cutting overhangs, branches lying on top of other branches. Deadwooding is straightforward; all dead limbs and branches have to go. And water sprouts and weed trees need to go. We make some sample cuts to show our volunteer apprentices. We select trees for them to work on, and they begin. And then they stop.

They ask me where to cut. Their fear is my own. I remember it; I was young, too, once: this turn, not that one; this cut means something is irrevocably lost, but something else gained.

I look at the tree, a lateral branch stretching across to nearly the next row as though it wants to know for certain that other trees like it do exist in this place. "Consider the whole tree," I tell the apprentices. "This is a tree that's lost its direction. It's going every which way. How can you redirect it? Ask yourself, and ask the tree." When did I learn this? Is it hubris to think these trees might teach, and in thinking so, that I have any role between teacher and disciple?

OBSCURANA, THE name Father Meyers and Victoria bestowed on our farm, means the place in the shadows, the hidden place, the hideaway. We don't use that name; we find it a little gloomy, like something out of a nineteenth-century German romance. But I cannot say that their story is over, that the rest is ours, mine and Gayle's, which we share with our family and friends. I used to daydream about starting fresh on clear land. I had no taste for living with other people's stuff, cleaning up other people's mess. And what would that have meant? No orchard, no cider. No pears, no peaches, no apricots, no plums. No roses. No fences, no barns, no pens, no henhouse. No gallery, no writing shed, no root cellar. And no place to live. Some friends who have struggled for twenty-five years on the kind of clear land I had envisioned are today far from having their place resemble their dreams.

On a shelf in Gayle's gallery is a small black-and-white photograph of a tall gray-bearded man in a gown with embroidered designs around the bottom, with a cape fringed on the shoulders, and a prayer shawl fringed on the ends. He is standing before a cross on a backdrop of striped woven rugs in the style of the Chimayo weavers. On the walls and on the floor are more woven rugs, Chimayo and perhaps Navajo. Candelabra holding many burning candles hang from the beams on both sides of him. He stands tall with a trace of a smile. Who could deny that, regardless of how he is remembered, this Reverend Friedrich Meyers was a handsome man? The photo has no date, only a title: "Rio Oscuro Chapel." It may well have been taken on the day he celebrated his first mass in his chapel, now this gallery.

BEFORE HE met Marni here at the farm on that early November weekend, Peter Keegan had planned Santa Fe as a stopover on his way to San Francisco. But his friend Sam had brought him to the Rio Oscuro Studio Tour, and so afterwards Peter detoured to Albuquerque to visit Marni. Then he went on. But he came back to Albuquerque the following week, looked for work in computer programming, found it, and settled in. In the winter Marni and Peter rented a house together on Morningside Street, Northeast. At its northern end, this section of Morningside stops at Lomas Boulevard, a major east-west artery. A large Roman Catholic church stands on the corner of Lomas and Morningside. Its southern end is at Central Avenue, once known as Route 66 and still occupied in part by motels going back to prefreeway times. Down Central to the west, less than a mile away, is the campus of the University of New Mexico with its unique neo-adobe architecture and large open spaces and an adjoining student and faculty community with restaurants, bookstores, and coffeehouses. The classrooms and laboratories of the Department of Psychology in which Marni was enrolled were in a traditional adobe-style building one block north of Central Avenue.

Up Central Avenue to the east were more motels and restaurants, a large office building, a large shopping center on a cross street, the New Mexico State Fairgrounds that hosted the spring and fall art shows Gayle exhibited in, the ten thousand–foot Sandia-Manzano Mountains at the eastern edge of the city, and, to the south, running up to and into the mountains, the sprawling Kirtland Air Force Base and within its boundaries the large fenced and guarded nuclear weapons laboratory where I had worked too many years.

Morningside between Central and Lomas and the streets east and west of it were quiet neighborhoods of well-kept small- and medium-size one-story houses, largely owner-occupied but some also rented to students. Down these quiet streets next year Marni would walk her baby in her stroller when she was feeling well enough, and Gayle and I would also walk him here when we came to visit. Marni and Peter's house had two bedrooms, a living room, a small kitchen with dining area, a laundry room leading to the backyard, and an enclosed garage. In front were two large blue spruces and in the back two full-size apple trees, a lawn, and plenty of sunny garden space. Marni loved it, a house of her own with a place for a garden.

Marni showed Peter the houses and neighborhoods where she had grown up. She showed him Valley High School where she had studied French and been inducted into the National Honor Society. She took him walking in the Rio Grande bosque that I had helped turn into a nature preserve, and hiking up into the Sandia Mountains where I had hiked often with her and her brothers and sister. In late winter when you followed the trail along the Embudito Creek on the west face of the Sandias you entered a land of rock faces masked with great sheets of ice, and beside them pussy willows ready to burst into blossom. Then you went higher through the patches of snow into the ponderosa forest, and the city that had been at your heels just a half hour ago was gone. You were in splendid wilderness with deer and even Rocky Mountain sheep, if you went to the right place. Yes, Marni had traveled in Europe and sailed in the Islands, but this was her home, her place. And Peter decided it should be his place, too, with her.

1991. MARNI and Peter had reserved the small Alumni Chapel on the University of New Mexico campus just down the road from their home for a spring wedding. They asked Barbara Pepper, a friend of Marni's who was a minister and also a midwife, to conduct the ceremony. They had invited Peter's family and friends from Pittsburgh and Boston and Los Angeles, Marni's family in New Mexico, and friends from Albuquerque. It was not to be a large wedding, but it would be on the formal side. As always, though, in everything Marni touched was the element of the unexpected, of possibility, even magic.

Now, the day of the wedding, Marni's mother, Dita, and I waited side by side in the small anteroom for the ceremony to begin. This was Marni's doing: since both of us had raised her, both of us would walk Marni down the aisle to present her to Peter. Dita and I had hardly spoken for years. Suddenly she turned to me and threw her arms around me. "We did it!" she said. Yes, we did, and I put my arms around her, for our daughter and for Peter and their possibilities. But I couldn't do anything for ours. Dita's hurts were too many and too deep to bandage, even temporarily, even if she would want it. She quickly backed away, and we carried on as if nothing had happened.

THESE DAYS my mind returns to the memory of those in that chapel in May, unsure of its reception, hesitant as a stray dog to an open hand—Marni and Peter; Dita; Barbara Pepper, the minister; the young women and young men of the wedding party. Peter slides the ring on Marni's finger and says the words we know by heart. In a restaurant six months before on her thirtieth birthday Marni had told Gayle she had met the man whom she would marry. I hear her and see her; she is radiant. Now it is coming to pass. How had she known? How had she recognized the one among strangers from that chance meeting at the farm during the art tour?

Stop. I want to stay in this moment in the chapel, to really see the look in my daughter's eyes. Yes, Marni, I want your whole wedding again, all the people, the music, the flowers, the toasting of you and Peter, dancing with you, all of it. You laugh. "Dad, don't be silly." But you see, Marni, while I am quick enough to grasp what is not very important, what has real meaning I am slow to appreciate. I am most comfortable with the tempo of trees, and the older the better. They don't move around, and I can go back for second looks. Your childhood was over so fast, your schooling abroad, and now your wedding, and the corsages and boutonnieres and all the flowers and all the smiles are gone to where smiles and flowers go. And never return.

IN JULY Marni called with some news: she was expecting. That was wonderful. The fall was a rich time of year for us, harvest, cider. October. Perfect. Two weeks later she called again. "Sit down, Dad," she said. "I have something to tell you. I have cancer, breast cancer. The doctor wants to operate right away, but we are going to get a second opinion."

THERE IS no easy time or season for truth-telling. First thing in the morning, for example. Go outside, hear the river. Then answer;

tell all the secrets before anyone else wakes up. Yes. Yet I can never be the first one awake on this farm. The salt-and-pepper rooster in the lower coop always beats me, and sometimes his Araucana father up here beats me too. And the guineas seem not to sleep at all. I have walked many times late at night under their roost in the big mulberry, and they are always whispering, murmuring, saying something softly. True, they are not bellowing as they do sometimes in the afternoons. This is gentle night-talk. Perhaps it is sleep-talk. I do not know about guineas, but I believe they must be awake to go on and on like that. Perhaps they are the only creatures in this creation who never sleep.

All right, forget the morning. How about midnight, midnight in the dead of winter. Now hear this. No. Why add to the burden of winter by dredging ancient ice out of the heart? Why spoil spring by unpacking old lies, broken covenants, betrayals of promises? Sadnesses? Griefs. Morning or midnight, it's always the same; we want to change the truth, change what we hear, and usually we try to change something or attain something without first finding out the meaning. We only pretend to be awake.

FEBRUARY, LATE afternoon, time to escort the geese back to their pen. When we are outside, we let them roam the road and the fields to glean what they can from last year's weeds. But when we cannot watch them, we put them inside the garden fence. Though it is possible for a coyote to jump that fence, it is not as easy an opportunity as a gaggle of fat Toulouse geese feeding in the open.

Last fall, after "our" gray coyote had taken yet another chicken, it established an observation post on the rocks at the edge of the mesa above the house. We looked at it, it looked at us, and waited, as if watching for an opportunity to come down to lunch. And, as if to add insult to injury, it barked. Finally Gayle got her pistol and shot at it. The bullet clipped the ground nearby. The coyote sat still on its haunches. She shot at it again. The bullet came closer, and this time, reluctantly, the coyote did move. Coyotes can be daring. I have seen a coyote run up our road, jump on a goose, and hold on while I shouted and ran toward it with a pitchfork and not let go till I was less than fifty feet away. Another coyote grabbed a goose swimming in the acequia just across the bridge from the front porch where we were sitting, and let go only when we and all the dogs ran after it.

But this coyote was still in no hurry. Finally, taking its own time, it stood up, turned, and walked away up mesa. We have not seen the gray coyote all winter. Perhaps one of the neighbors shot it. Or it might even right now be up there, watching.

I open the garden gate now so the geese can go back to their pen for the night. They are not interested in leaving, not just now, thank you, and they pay me no mind. All right. I go inside the fence, slowly, deliberately, not wanting them to panic. Now they begin their waddling, all in a bunch, but poorly aimed so that two of them run right into the fence. They turn left and find themselves in a blind corner that causes all of them to get upset and make a racket as though something were out to get them. I walk behind the misdirected, and they try again and make it out the gate this time. Now they rejoin the gaggle, and all waddle down through the grapes, turning at the old Lincoln pear, stopping: another obstacle, the lateral ditch, just a foot across but very deep. The two tall white geese honk, flap their wings with great determination, and make it to the other side. A big Toulouse follows. The next one trips and slides into the ditch and then begins flapping and honking with so much frenzy one might think all the coyotes of hell are after her. Finally she beats her way out of the ditch and onto the road. When the last goose reaches the road they all take off down hill, flapping wings, honking, running, churning up the dust. For a hundred feet the geese beat the air furiously, and some even get off the ground! But then, just as suddenly as they started, they stop, their springs all unwound, and they waddle through their home gate into the pen.

I close in the geese and close in the chickens and start up the hill to finish the evening chores. It is quiet, the late winter afternoon quiet, no bees, no summer smells, the farm and the trees still, the air now cooling as the sun goes behind the hill. The snow clings to the north-facing slope in front of me between the juniper and piñon. Below the ditch are more patches of snow. Snow and ice still cover the stone stairway and the ground and the walk, and whatever else the house still shadows. Even with warm days the winter ice has a way of clinging to its positions, almost as though it thinks of staying forever.

At the top of the bank, just out from under the third willow, on the bridge over the acequia, there I hear them. I stop. I hear them again, faintly, just loud enough. I look up. There they are, a great living, waving wedge, a flapping white-and-gold vee swimming through the slanting sun and scattering its rays in waves across the sky.

Half my life I have attended these birds, these creatures that follow the Rio Grande south in the fall and north in the spring. I have heard their calls through windows and doors and even through adobe walls. They announce the seasons. They give directions, the important ones: pole to pole. They tell all who will listen that the planet, in spite of all we have done, still lives, still teems with life.

This first band is high. They vee over the river and then over the seven thousand–foot mesa with thousands of feet to spare, as though they had set their northerly course when they left the refuge three hundred miles ago and knew then exactly what they would find and where. How they do it seems a miracle. Wild geese. They have organization that goes back beyond time. They have purpose, direction. They have leaders, unity. They make common cause as second nature. How are these called wild, when we with no purpose, no direction, no leaders, no unity, and certainly no common cause call ourselves civilized?

I put my hands to my eyes to hold their driving, weaving trail in my sight. I follow them over Black Mesa, heading toward Colorado, Canada, Alaska. They pull me northward. I stretch, I strain. Slowly, imperceptibly, they merge with the blue, with the white haze, become less and less separate and more and more part of the whole. I blink and peer, and blink. There, there, no, there, there! Until finally they are nowhere.

I look up at the mesa. The snow is holding on in the north-facing slope, holding fast to the rocks and the greasewood, the junipers, the piñon, the chamisa and sage. The snow is holding fast in the orchard, on the ground, on the trees, on the fence posts, on the roof of the pole barn, holding fast. And the horses wait in the snow, unwilling to wait in the barn, standing outside at night as the snow falls on them, waiting for it to fall, waiting for it to stop, waiting for day, waiting for me to come with hay, to break the ice on their water, waiting, steaming, standing still, even as they move through the snow, the white face and the brown face.

But I have heard the geese flying north.

BOOK 2

The Cidermaster's

Handbook

PART 3

Keeping the Record

*Seasons move like a river with high water
and low water, yet without seams. We note
the seasons and fit our lives into them as we can.*
THE CIDERMASTER'S HANDBOOK

ABIDE.

But nothing abides.

Earth turns. Ice melts. Our hill melts. Horses begin to shed their winter coats. End of March and the first apricots blossom.

Orchard grass greens. Apricots swell. We clean Acequia Ultima. Rain. Rain on the mountains, rain on the mesas, rain on our hill. Water in the root cellar despite the new wall. Water in the writing house because flowing water could not find a drain built to convey the water, however hard it looked. And the mountain moves.

The mountain moves. Build a house on sand and the river washes it away. Build a house on rock, anchor it to the bedrock. Be sure, be firm. Mountain moves, bedrock moves.

Nothing abides. Not passion, not life. Foothill creeps, covers roof of hidden room, roof gives way, foothill sifts in, then pours in, burying further the buried treasure in the back of the stone barn, if there is a treasure buried and if it is buried there.

Hold on.

SATURDAY MORNING, and Monte is ready to work, just as he had promised. In one hand he holds a new pair of suede work gloves, in the other the handle of a new shovel. I admire the shovel—the straight, pointed ditch blade, the red-and-green label on the blade, the long polished handle with "24.95" written with felt-tipped marker and "Tru-Temper" burned into the wood.

Of all the friends who have come to help, Monte is the first person to come with his own tool, and a brand new one at that. "Where do you want me to start?"

We had finished the spring cleaning of the main laterals and let in the first water. The grapes were left, the three long rows of overgrown, weed-covered vines that we had barely touched last year. Last year the old water furrows were so overgrown and so pocked with gopher holes that the water never made it beyond the upper half of Father Meyers's vineyard. Each year I vowed to run water the full length, and each year the gophers intervened. I would fill one hole, tamp it, put the water back in the furrow, and leave. An hour or two later I would check again, and the water would be pouring down the bank from another hole.

After Friedrich Meyers died, and there was no longer the pressing need to make those barrels of sweet wine, Victoria and Corina had probably given up on this vineyard. Half of every summer I fought the gophers, then I gave up. I cut into the middle of the vineyard and irrigated the lower half from another lateral. But now, with Monte and his new shovel, we have a chance to get to the end.

I start raking out the grass and weeds and dead leaves and cutting and pulling out the dead vines. Monte digs out the feeder ditch along the chicken and goose pens. He moves backwards, one shovel-cut at a time. Every few yards he stops, steps forward, cleans out the loose dirt, then moves on. He works the shovel as deftly as if it were a pencil working over a rough draft one of his staff has left on his desk. Shovel-cut by shovel-cut he moves along the fence, under the great pear tree. Each bite is the same size as the one before. In his hands the shovel seems less like the humble tool it is and more like a precision instrument to set right this ditch, this farm.

He finishes the ditch. We start the new furrows for the grapes. We stop for lunch with Gayle and Julia, Monte's wife, who have been painting in the orchard. Then back to the shovels, Monte's pointed true temper, my worn, rounded, often-sharpened old slogger. We cut weeds, branches, roots. We fill holes. We move earth. At five o'clock we put in the water. I watch it for a while, then follow Monte up to the house. On this day I am too tired to care what happens with the gophers.

MEMBERS OF Acequia associations in northern New Mexico have been cutting back the willows and shoveling out the silt and leaves in the spring for hundreds of years. When the rivers rise, we keep watch at the headgates to pull out the logs and branches that come down from the mountains. When the river falls we wade out to put big rocks into the main channel to get more water to our heading. All this hand and shovel work is observed and described as our keeping faith with our culture, our traditions.

This is the historical perspective, at any rate. For us and our neighbors, however, the reason for working on the ditch is much simpler. Without the acequias we would have no gardens or orchards or vineyards, no fields of corn and chile and squash, no alfalfa for our animals. We may argue about who will clean or repair the acequia, or how it should be done, but seldom about why.

In Zen terms cleaning the acequia each spring might be considered communal meditation. We are not trying to change anything, or attain something special; we are simply cutting weeds and shoveling dirt.

At seven-thirty in the morning the peones, or workers, gather at the headgate. Each peon tells the mayordomo which parciante, or landowner, he or she will be working for. The mayordomo gives each one a number. When everyone has signed up the mayordomo gets into the acequia and starts marking off the tareas, six- or seven-foot work sections, calling out "Uno! Dos! Tres!" as he marks boundaries in the dirt. Now the peones begin cutting and shoveling. When they are done, they wait for the mayordomo to inspect the work. Then the mayordomo marks the next tareas. All day long, from eight in the morning till five, mark the tarea, shovel it out, wait, then begin again. Sometimes deeper, sometimes wider, but always straight on. If not enough workers show up, it may take a second day.

At the end of the day the worker will get a slip addressed to his parciante stating hours worked and money owed. The parciante then pays his worker. First-time peones, those who have never cleaned any acequia and also never talked to anyone who has, cannot know when they start in the early morning what will be asked of them that day. And their shovels may be unfamiliar to their hands. But by the end of the day, at the end of walking and shoveling almost three miles, they usually know in their bodies that they have accomplished something. Many come back year after year. When an old-timer does not show up one spring, we talk about him, remembering him and his shovel.

IN NORTHERN New Mexico acequias have been in use for hundreds of years. The word *acequia* is Arabic. It came into the Spanish language a thousand years ago during the occupation of Spain by the Moors. The Spanish carried the term to the Southwest and applied it to the existing Native American irrigation systems. And as they moved into the high, narrow mountain valleys beyond the native villages, clearing new land for cultivation and homes, the settlers carved out new acequias—around hillsides, down mountains, through forests, over ravines and arroyos and flowing streams. Their tools were shovels and picks and sometimes scoops pulled by horses. They hollowed logs to span gullies and ravines. They used simple water levels to make sure the grade was always downhill. And their work made the land fruitful.

In the northern counties today—Rio Arriba, Taos, Mora, and elsewhere, too—farmers, however long they have lived on and worked their lands, depend on their acequias just as much as the first settlers. Each registered acequia is a political entity operated by its shareholders under bylaws they have adopted in accordance with state law. State laws protect acequia rights, and, where necessary, the state court system enforces acequia rulings. In many rural communities residents depend on their elected acequia commissioners, the only elected local officials, for help with more than water. And cleaning acequias every spring has always been, and still is, an important community activity.

I have served as an acequia commissioner for twelve years. Our neighbor Clovis Romero, who also grows apples, has served for more than thirty years. His experience with our acequia is an invaluable resource for the community. Of our thirty-five parciantes, a good three-quarters are descendants of original Spanish settlers. But however long we have lived on our lands, we all have the same opportunity to be keepers and caretakers, to enrich our own lives and those of our neighbors and their children and ours in ways that have real meaning.

Carl Tsosie, a tribal officer of Picuris Pueblo, addressed the issue of caretaking at a meeting of the Rio Pueblo–Rio Oscuro watershed coalition. Pueblo Indians are tied to their land, he said; it is their home, their life, their religion. And they have been on the land forever. "But now it does not matter how long you have been here or where you have come from. We are all here now, and we all have to take care of our land and our water together. We cannot keep moving to another place because we have not taken care of what we had. There is no other place. This place is all we have now."

SOME DAYS I walk silently through the orchard in the early morning counting my breaths in a walking meditation. On these mornings I do not walk to recognize or name, to check or smell, or to remember. Yes, I see—manure, branches down, holes, dead limbs, water, mud, tall grass, a jungle of young willows, poplars, elms, flowers, more mud. But now I am just walking to be with myself.

I slip through the fence by the old fruit stand, see the newspaper in the box and consciously do not reach for it, now follow the road toward the hill, keeping myself and the whole farm in place, breathing, counting my breaths.

Though Victoria and Corina and Annelise buried Friedrich Meyers in his cemetery on Barrancos Blancos, they kept his room, his bed, his books, his creed, his surplices ready so that at any moment he might come back and say mass in his chapel again on the last day—and go down to the shed and start up the old Ford 8N and disk the orchard on the day after.

We hold on. We hold on to what we have. We fight water, we fight dirt, we fight for life. We hold on until all we have is the holding on.

FATHER MEYERS was superintendent of the public schools in Rio Oscuro, and his nuns taught there. (Non-Catholics eventually sued to get the nuns out. The court ruled they could stay, but they could not wear their habits in class or give religious instruction in the classroom.) According to an old grade book we found in the garage, Corina Coronada attended Rio Oscuro Public Schools from 1927 to 1930. Sister Mary Lorraine Gibson was her homeroom teacher in 1927. She received a C in world history, a B in general science, a C in algebra, and a C in English. She attended 150 1/2 days out of 180. The class had twelve students, ages fourteen to eighteen; Corina was eighteen. In her final year her grades were D- in English and Spanish, C+ in typewriting, D+ in shorthand, and D in business arithmetic, with perfect attendance.

She came to the farm as a housekeeper right out of school and never left for fifty years. Toward the end, with Father Meyers and Anna Schaffle long gone and Victoria Howser less and less able to get around, tiny Corina, now in her seventies, took over the farmwork as best she could, fed chickens and rabbits, planted tomatoes, and did the nursing. And thus she became principal beneficiary in Victoria's will.

In the spring after we moved in I went to see Corina. She had called about a sickle that she had left behind and wanted back. I had found two in the shed, a fairly new one and the other almost rusted through and held together by bailing wire. I brought the good one. She was living in a small house in the village that belonged to her niece. Corina was out back, at the edge of a tilled field. She was sitting in a chair watching the water run into some new furrows. I handed her the sickle. "Snow peas," she said, pointing to the first leaves, "and early lettuce." The water moved very slowly, more a trickle than a flow. "When I finish the watering, I will show you the house." I watched the water with her. As each furrow filled with water she would close it and open the next. When all the rows were soaked she closed the water gate, and we walked around the house.

She moved slowly, as though in the months since she had left the farm and its long drive and large orchard and many buildings she had gotten out of the habit of walking any distance. Her garden was right out back, and her niece's house was but a few steps away. We came to a storage shed, and Corina opened the door. I stood there beside her, looking, not sure what she wanted me to do or say. The shed was packed: boxes and clothes and curtains on top of the boxes, a lamp, a broken chair, a coil spring and a mattress, and more things I could not distinguish in the back. These were some of the things her family had helped her move from the farm. "This is all my stuff," she said. I could not tell by her tone whether she was pleased to own all of it or bewildered as to what she would do with it. Fifty years she had been taking care of Father Meyers and Victoria and their household and all its secrets. For the last twenty years the household was just her and Victoria. Now everyone was gone, and the farm, and all she had to take care of were these things and the memories and the secrets.

Corina's small adobe house was like the shed, only larger and with windows. Every foot of the living room was packed from floor to ceiling with furniture and furnishings, save for a narrow corridor that led to the kitchen. The movers—her nieces and their husbands and children—had stacked her boxes wherever there was space. These were the treasures she guarded now, and they took up almost all of her living space.

"Do you want some tea?" she said as we stood there in the corridor. "I'm sorry I can't ask you to sit down, but there is no place."

"That's all right, I have to get back. You had wanted to come over and pick some apricots."

"Yes, and later some grapes."

"I think we'll have plenty of apricots this year," I said. "I'll let you know when they're ready."

Now she looked at the sickle I had brought. She looked at me. "There was another one. I used it to cut grass for the rabbits."

I looked at her. The other sickle. The one so rusted it would cut nothing. But she wanted it, too. "I'll look around," I said.

And I left her there in the middle of her things. I had lied. I knew where that other sickle was, but I had no intention of taking it to her; I was going to throw it away. That was one less thing she would have to worry about.

Corina was not poor. She had a place to live, and she had money, 40 percent of Victoria's estate. But she was in her seventies, probably too late to get into the habit of spending on herself when she had lived all her life on the farm taking care of others and just making do. She, who had always saved seeds, could now buy all she wanted for her garden, and all the food a tiny woman living alone could make use of, plus the tea and cookies she might want to offer visitors as she used to do at the farm, if she could find someplace here for them to sit.

Yet I could have been all wrong about Corina and what she might do. Maybe she would sell her stuff or give it away, maybe spend money on her grandnieces and -nephews, maybe she would even make a trip to California to visit the nieces and nephews of Victoria who used to come to the farm when they were young. I got into the truck, and Corina came outside. I waved to her. She lifted her hand and waved back with her small fingers, a thin, tiny woman darkened by age and the sun, standing there by her house alone.

When the apricots were ripe I did call Corina's niece and asked her to relay the message. But Corina never came to pick apricots, and I never saw her again.

AMONG THE riches of the farm were the pocket vineyards spliced into slopes and corners above the main orchard, three long rows terraced into the hill above the apricots, three short rows between the road and the strawberries, a row lost in a thicket of wild roses, a row hidden among the cherries, another tucked in with apples and pears, and remnants of vines all but shaded away by flowering quince and bridal wreath. We know that Father Meyers liked his wine and his spirits. But I wonder now whether this seemingly random placement of vineyards also had meaning. If I plotted them on a map would we see a pattern? A cross? A prayer sign to Our Lady of the Orchard or a native harvest deity? Or a wink to Bacchus and Apollo?

But meaning or not we abounded in grapes. In the first years Gayle and I filled box after box with the purple Concord, red Carmine, and white Niagara. I took most of the boxes to farmers' markets for juice makers and wine makers and others who just enjoyed old-fashioned unsprayed grapes and did not mind the seeds. And with the Carmine grapes Gayle made wine, a dry ruby table wine that she served at special occasions.

When we arrived the vineyards had not been tended for many years, and, like many other untended things, the grapes had returned to directions and shapes encoded in their genes. New vines and ancient ones, the living and the dead, wound and wound around each other in an intimate, multigenerational support system. Each trunk cluster was a family, partners and offspring who had lived together so long and interchanged so many habits and judgments it would challenge the most astute marriage counselor to find ways to identify individualities. Such interdependence was undreamed of by the writers of pamphlets on pruning grapes passed out by the agricultural extension service. Either that or they chose to ignore such real chaos and deal with the linear fiction of simple plants with three simple runners to be tied to three simple wires that could be sketched in three minutes. Then they went on to more favored topics, topics like the benefits of chemical fertilizers and the use of chemicals to protect the grape from life-forms at lower levels on the great chain of being.

If I were Victoria in her nineties, I would not consider pruning these vineyards. Certainly not with everything else there was to do. And why prune anyway, with such good harvests? Well, in some sections in some rows the dead vines had begun to choke the life out of the living. And vines were climbing into the good Lincoln pears and strangling them. Clearly the vineyards had a good claim for our attention.

I SEE Marni in the vineyard. Marni came up to help prune the grapes in 1990 during spring break at the University of New Mexico. Besides enjoying the farm and farming in general, she seemed to have had an affinity for grapes that went back to her childhood. She had a taste for grape leaves, and for her birthday luncheons she wanted to be taken to restaurants that offered dolmas. And she liked to taste wine whenever it was on the dinner table. Perhaps this had something to do with a Romanian great-grandfather, my mother's father, in her gene pool. According to my aunt, each year Julius Marcus would buy a ton of red and a half ton of white grapes to make wine in his basement. His wine was known throughout the neighborhood, and his friends considered it a great honor to be given a bottle of good Marcus wine.

Marni furthered her interest in grapes and farming during the year she studied French in Neuchâtel. In the fall she went with a group of Swiss students to harvest grapes in France. For half that year her Swiss host family were townspeople. Then she moved in with a young farming couple in the mountains, and helped care for their baby and their calves. She came back fluent enough in French that after taking one French-language course, the University of New Mexico gave her credit for a minor in the language.

We started with the single row of grapes at the top of the slope, an impenetrable tangle of vines. "What shall we do with that?" I asked.

She bent over to inspect the first trunk. Her long brown hair fell over her face. She separated the branches with her slender fingers as though to audition them for a performance in a new dance. She smiled, the small smile of her inner self that had been Marni since she was a young girl.

"Let's see," she said, "if we give you the lead, how will that work?" She ran her fingers up the trunk and along one vine, letting her muse connect with the art of the vine, feeling out what would work, what would be right. "Yes, you will do." She positioned the jaws of the clipper. She cut. I pulled out the pruned one, dragged it to the road. Then the next, and the next. We stepped back. Three leaders and light, light in between!

We pruned the row, feeling our way, auditioning, cutting, separating, pulling out the dead and the superfluous, raking out the leaves and silt, and finally tightening the wires and tying the keepers in their new places. I liked the way Marni worked, her grace in handling the vines, her decisiveness in picking what to keep, her sureness in cutting. I liked working with her. I liked watching her.

Marni moved, and had moved even as a child, with a certain presence, as though she always knew exactly where she was going even if she had never been there before. Perhaps it was her smile, just the trace of a smile that seemed to say *I know who I am.* I once saw that same smile in a photograph of Marni's mother at ten. I think the photo was taken by Dita's father after Dita had just run a race. Dita's hair was braided, and her eyes and jaw were different. But the expression, the smile, was the same as Marni's.

One time I caught Marni's smile as she ran past us and scampered up the washed-out trail to the Acomas' Enchanted Mesa.

Marni was about eight. Dita's mother was visiting us from Germany. She called out, *"Nein, nein! Das is zu gefährlich!"* But Marni kept going, so we sent her brother Andrew after her to make sure she was all right. And then I followed, a little more slowly. I remember Marni in her ballet costume, on stage, dancing, smiling. And on stage in the high school play, *The Effect of Gamma Rays on Man in the Moon Marigolds,* perfectly fitting the part of the slender girl transformed. And she was no wimp. On my fiftieth birthday, the day after she came home from Switzerland, I asked her and Andrew to climb with me up the steep Sandia wilderness trail all the way to the ten thousand–foot south peak. We did that.

I wished she could stay now, but that was not the way it would be. The farm was Gayle's and mine, our project, our risk, our responsibility. Her children and mine all helped, as they could, when it worked out. Our wanting them to visit and their wanting to visit were balanced by their own needs, their friends and families, their lives.

We waved good-bye, and she drove her tan pickup down the drive and out of sight.

IN THE spring we shovel last year's silt and rocks and roots and leaves out of the communal acequia and our own ditches to clear the way for the new water for our fields and orchards. In the summer, in the monsoon season, a heavy, black storm cloud will sometimes find our mesa and hover, as though held in place by an ancient rain dance, and pour and pour on the plains and slopes of basalt and sage and juniper and piñon until a great churning, silt-laden flood roars down our arroyo and fills the acequia and our ditches with ten times more silt than we shoveled out in the spring. Then the clouds pass, the unrelenting mountain sun comes out, dries the leaves and the ground, and the orchard wants its regular water; so we shovel out the ditches again.

Not every summer rain brings down silt. In sun showers or long, gentle rains, the water sinks into the slopes. And we may go one, two, or three summers without a rain heavy enough to move silt. A heavy storm may center up the road or just across the river or a mile beyond, and we learn of it when the river rises and turns brown. But eventually our turn comes; the black rain cloud mounts our mesa. And worse still is the summer this happens more than once.

Sometimes during particularly long days of shoveling out whole hills of runoff silt I wonder if this small work could possibly count as penance. Penance, however small or partial, for my part in the ripping of a thousand holes and tunnels into the desert plains and mountains of Nevada? I forgive the violence of the storm, nature; I have no choice. But will nature forgive me?

Chilean poet and Nobel laureate Pablo Neruda once described himself as a man named Pablo who had love, doubts, and debts, *amor, dudas, deudas*. Neruda is reportedly the most widely published poet of the twentieth century, with giant editions in Chinese and Russian as well as Spanish. I cannot speak for any other of his millions of readers, but I accept that summation for myself. *Yo me llamo* Harvey, *tengo dudas, tengo deudas,* and I shovel, and I shovel.

I got to the nuclear weapons testing program in Nevada by way of the job I took in Albuquerque in 1961 after being a college instructor for two years in Flagstaff. I started at the Sandia weapons-design laboratory as a technical writer. Sandia was at the center of Cold War nuclear weapons development, a key facility in our strategy of using mutual guaranteed destruction as the path to peace, and along the way the laboratory hired dozens of poets and writers and college English teachers to help its engineers and scientists organize their data and graphics and write purpose statements, introductions, conclusions, and summaries. Sometimes we worked on quarterly reports and annual reports. Occasionally I wrote speeches and articles for our department manager who was interested in the environment: "Save the Grand Canyon for Our Grandchildren," "The Value of Grasslands," "The Bosque Is Our Heritage." We were all paid more than poets and English teachers usually make, and besides that we had health insurance, tuition assistance if we wanted to continue schooling, and four-week vacations. Some had taken tech-writing jobs as an alternative to teaching, and some were pursuing doctoral degrees and intended to return to teaching when they graduated.

For anyone who had taught college composition, the job of helping engineers with their reports was not particularly challenging. But Charlie, who had had a doctoral dissertation on Daniel Defoe under way for years, and was our de facto English professor in residence, had another purpose. Whether it was about Eliot, Marvel, or Milton, Hardy, Hawthorne, or Melville, or any contemporary writer, I found Charlie knowledgeable and enthusiastic. I had met him at the University of Iowa and kept in contact while I was teaching in Flagstaff. I went to the lab partly so we could do a paper together on *Billy Budd* and Melville's concept of truth, veritas. And more than that I had missed and wanted the stimulation of talking with him.

Above Charlie's desk in our tech-writing offices he had a blackboard on which he tracked the progress of his reports. On the same board he wrote lists of books and writers. I know Thomas Hardy was on that list, and probably Henry Fielding and Daniel Defoe, and the books and the writers kept changing. The books were Charlie's interests, and the list was also his hook. All an engineering client had to do was ask a question about the list to get Charlie to recommend a reading program. Never did I see anything related to the mission of our national laboratory on those lists, but in a larger sense, of course, the lists were relevant, as reading literature is relevant to enlarging human consciousness, which cannot help but make us better engineers and better people.

But we were all mavericks, humanities types in laboratories of physicists, mathematicians, engineers, and technicians. To keep a foot in the teaching world and to earn a little extra money, many of us taught noon-hour and after-work and evening courses in speech, composition, technical writing, speed-reading, and critical reading. Unless there was a publication deadline, our editing was done in a leisurely fashion, and we had time to read and talk.

I remember conversations about achieving ultimate inner peace and preparing for an afterlife, if there was an afterlife, with Jack, a coworker who claimed to be a practicing Buddhist. Matt, a poet, talked about his math courses; to him math was "just like poetry." One thing we all agreed on, except for one person, was the good life outdoors in New Mexico. We talked about camping and hiking and working on gardens and lawns. Lloyd, the lone dissenter, had grown up on a dairy farm in the East. Lloyd read all the time, and he was a pleasure to talk to about books. But he had nothing to say about the great outdoors. Once and only one time I brought up my desire to live with the land instead of just sitting on it, and I asked about his experiences.

"I had to milk them and feed them every day before I went to school," he said. "It was always raining; there was always mud. I never stopped being wet and cold until I left home." He looked at me. "You wanted to know. That's what it was like." He spent as little time as possible outdoors, he said. His lawn mower was broken, and he wasn't planning to get it fixed.

My clients were mostly engineers who designed sensors, switches, controls, and safety devices and tested them in Nevada. I remember traveling to the Nevada testing site with Harry Kinney, an engineer who was also a Bernalillo County commissioner and was later elected mayor of Albuquerque. Harry, a political conservative, would come over at election time to what he probably considered the den of iniquity, the offices of the intellectual, professorial, nonconformist oddballs, to ask for our votes. "I think I know who will get your vote for governor," he said one time when Jack the Buddhist and I were in the office.

"No, Harry, you don't," said Jack.

"Jack's an anarchist," I said. "And he believes all politicians are servants of Satan and will have their just reward in hell." Harry smiled and we laughed.

"First of all," Jack said, "I don't believe in hell or Satan."

"Do you think you might consider voting for me for commissioner?" Harry said. He gave us election cards, and we thanked him. And I did vote for him because he was conscientious. When his first wife died he married Carol, who had shown a strong interest in the environment when she was a Los Alamos County commissioner. Eventually, as mayor of Albuquerque, long after I had left the lab and moved to the farm, Harry was instrumental in establishing an open-space division in city government that preserved and managed fifteen thousand acres of open mesa river woodland (the Bosque Nature Preserve), and a section of the Sandia Mountains that went all the way up to the ten thousand–foot crest. Harry appointed as open-space superintendent Rex Funk, our first pear picker on the farm. As a teacher in the Albuquerque Public Schools, Rex had promoted environmental education and helped form an association of environmental educators. As superintendent his continuing emphasis on education and public involvement in open-space preservation helped win the city a national environmental award. He also found himself taking a moderating position between developers, who wanted to block some trails and chip away fringes of open space for subdivisions and shopping centers, and environmental and preservation-minded citizens, who wanted to protect and expand open space.

"There's never an end to the development proposals that come across my desk," Rex told me once. "And some of the people I used to work with have accused me of selling out."

"And Mayor Harry?"

"So far he backs me up. The support from his wife doesn't hurt either."

Two elections later, when Harry was no longer in office and a strongly prodevelopment mayor took over, Rex decided it was time to retire.

Working with the mavericks at the laboratory was a good life for me, just so long as I didn't think about the consequences, the by-products, and, ultimately, the utter waste and futility of our work. But I couldn't not think about these things.

LAS VEGAS, six in the morning. Harry Kinney and Jim, a new tech writer, and I drive out into the desert toward the test site.

We say nothing. I try to focus. The screen of my mind's eye is a double exposure: the first light of dawn, the road, the blur of sand and cactus superimposed on the spotlights and stages and performers of the tour Harry gave us last night. Harry knew exactly where we should go for food, for glitter, for shows, for combos, for last drinks. Harry knew the performers, knew musicians, and introduced us. He kept asking how we were doing, whether there was anything special we wanted to see. Harry engineer, Harry host, Harry people person. I ease back in the seat, relax, close my eyes.

The car slows down and I sit up. We approach a fence, a gate, a guard. Harry stops, opens the window, and we hand out our badges. The guard is an older man with the dark, weathered face of a rancher; perhaps he has a small ranch and runs cattle in his off-hours. Or maybe his ranch is one of those taken over by the test range. He looks us over, hands back the badges, says nothing I can hear, and turns back to the guard shack. We drive into the compound, and the military gray drabness erases from my screen whatever residual glitter remains from last night, and now, ever so slowly, I begin to think about what I am supposed to be doing here, the information I am supposed to gather for the reports I will edit and help publish. We meet Bill, the testing technician Harry works with, and all four of us drive into the desert to a new steel superstructure surrounded by a cluster of trailers.

"This is the top of the mine shaft," Harry says. "Here we get the mine elevator that will take us down to the excavation."

We wait for the elevator, and I make a mental note: I have seen a mine shaft and a mine elevator and coal miners in the Saarland. And many pictures of mines. This is not a mine, not a mine shaft. The elevator comes up. It is a steel frame with a steel floor with no sides and no roof. We start down, down. Note: wherever we are going, we are not going into a drift of coal or diamonds or any lode of good minerals miners spend their lives removing from the earth.

The tunnel. A jumble of timber and metal, lights, wire, and cable running seemingly without direction. We walk. We follow

Bill and Harry. I glance at Jim, a poet, an English teacher; does he think, I want to ask, that if we keep walking here under the Channel we will reach France? Or are we just going under the Mississippi from Illinois to Iowa? Surely this must be part of some great undertaking, a tunnel like this, all this effort of excavation and structural support, illumination and atmospheric control. Under the Hudson River, at least. But Jim is in his own thoughts. I do not share my empty feeling about all this work for a one-time use, all this money we are spending.

We walk through the tunnel perhaps a quarter mile between bundles of cable, past technicians kneeling, bending over, reaching up from ladders to emplace and position experiments, check connections, pull wires into bundles. Harry stops. He points; this experiment is his. He talks with Bill and Jim, and I get as close as we can to the box fastened to the wall with all the wires coming out of it. The principle is simple: determine if the component will function in a nuclear explosion environment by exposing it to a nuclear explosion. Just how you do the measurements and how you interpret the results are the subjects of this experiment and of the reports we will be preparing.

We look past Bill and Harry to the end of the tunnel, to a chain-link fence and armed guards. Harry sees us looking. "The device is down there," Harry says. "Only the explosives people are allowed in." Which is fine with me; I am not interested in having a close-up look at a megaton nuclear warhead, let alone having a detailed explanation as to how it works.

We wait. Harry asks questions and Bill answers. Bill pulls out some drawings, and he shows them to Harry. Then, out of courtesy, he shows these drawings to us. At least one of the drawings will go into the report Jim will work on. Harry nods; he is satisfied. We walk back to the elevator. I turn around, look down the tunnel once more, the steel supports, the lights, the cables, and all the men working. I wonder, what was here before the digging? I cannot imagine this being *sipapu*, the hole in the earth where the ancestors of the Hopi and the Picuris and other Pueblo peoples came from, but I do not know for certain. And the operators of backhoes and front-end loaders and the other excavating equipment—they would have no way of knowing if what they dug out here was primordial, was the earth from which gods made men, sacred earth. I wonder who would know. Not a geologist, not an anthropologist, not a microbiologist. Maybe a medicine man. Good-bye, I say softly to the tunnel and whomever and whatever is listening. I step into the elevator, Bill shuts the door, and we start up toward the surface.

On the surface, fresh air, sunlight. We walk over to one of the aluminum instrument trailers. Inside are racks of oscilloscopes connected to the ends of the cables that connect to experiments in the tunnel. And in front of the oscilloscopes are ultrahigh-speed cameras with microsecond and picosecond response times. Harry tells Jim and me what kind of data he will be looking for. Bill answers questions. Harry finds everything in order. Timetable: two weeks to finish installing experiments and three weeks to evacuate, close, and seal, then apply to Washington for approval to fire. Then analyze results. Then decide: if Harry's component survives the test exposure long enough to function it is therefore suitable for incorporation in nuclear weapon X now being developed at the laboratory. Eventually the component will go to a manufacturer for production and then, along with all the other components and systems tested and proven and manufactured, will be assembled into the final weapon. If the test results are ambiguous or unsatisfactory, Harry and his colleagues will analyze the problem, rework the component, and test it again.

Final weapons, ready to deploy, are put in stockpile or in a readiness position. The details of design and deployment, of course, are all secret. What is not secret is the fact that we have these weapons in our arsenal. This is the principle of nuclear deterrence, of peacekeeping by deterrence, the policy of mutual sustained terror; if each adversary knows the other has terrible weapons, then neither will use them. And sometime in the future, when the adversaries come to their senses, weapons will be destroyed. In the meantime, design, development, and testing will continue. And the hope, and trust, of all sane peoples in all nations is that these weapons must not, cannot, will not ever be used. On some days I think of this policy as mutual schizophrenia.

And it is also potlatching, but on a global scale. We build and test and stockpile to eventually destroy and throw away what we have spent our wealth on, and the adversary builds and tests and stockpiles to eventually destroy and throw away in a great contest to see who can spend and throw away the most without totally bankrupting the supporting economy first. We are convinced that whatever social cost to us, we will win; our economy, our economic system, our society can support more building and then throwing away than that of the adversary. Whatever the cost, at any cost, we will win. And here am I at the Nevada testing site, part of the program sustaining this madness.

NOON. WE get sandwiches at the cafeteria and head out into the desert toward another area and a shot scheduled for this afternoon. The testing site is a vast arid range of plains and hills and mountains and a western desert biota—coyotes, rabbits, snakes, scorpions, antelope, and the thousands upon thousands of spiders and ants and flying insects and the cacti and herbs and shrubs they pollinate and feed upon. Before the test site there was a gunnery range. Before that ranches and cattle. Before that Native American hunters. Now, even if the ranchers or the Native Americans could get back this land, they might have a hard time dealing with the changes, the great landmarks—or, rather, marks in the land. And the genetic changes and mutations in plant life and animal life from prolonged exposure to radiation. Studies of such changes in humans are only now beginning. Studying radiation effects on flora and fauna in the desert has a lower funding priority.

We drive ten, maybe fifteen miles, and Harry stops. We get out. We look into a depression as wide as a city block, maybe twice as wide, as deep as I remember Meteor Crater in Arizona, but it is not a body from outer space that is buried here.

"Sudan," Harry says; "the first nuclear test underground. A

megaton." Jim and I look. And before underground testing, everything went up, to come down we know not where, or so we once pretended. I say none of this, however.

We drive on. Other depressions, other markers. Harry calls out the names of tests, "events," as we pass. The dirt road drops into an arroyo. A jackrabbit jumps out from behind a rock, and Harry brakes. It crosses the road and runs up the bank. The road turns around one hill and then another. Then we turn up to a fenced compound, stop at the guard post, and hand out our badges. The guard says he'll be closing this gate in half an hour and waves us through.

While component designers are concerned about function and survivability, physicists measure weapon yields, the explosive force, to verify conformance of their devices to the design requirements. And the performance of the underground testing system must also be verified by engineers and managers up to the director of the test site, the president of the laboratory, and all the way to the head of the energy agency in Washington. Once the device detonates and the sensors transmit their data about yield and function and survival, the covers must instantly seal the tunnel so that absolutely no particles, not the slightest measurable radioactivity, escapes to the atmosphere. The whole world will know of an underground nuclear test, whether Washington announces it or not, because the detonation is a seismic event recorded at earthquake-watch stations around the globe. But announcement by venting, by the escape of any radioactivity because of a flawed capping system, is an occurrence of grave consequence, one to be fervently avoided. We know more than we wish to know about exposure to radioactive fallout. Containment is what underground testing is all about, containment of death, "harmless" containment in the earth.

We drive uphill to the operations bunker, a reinforced concrete building with tiny windows and a steel door. At the door another guard checks our badges. Harry shows us the test control room, introduces us to people at control panels—"Jim, our new tech writer, and Harvey." Smile, shake hands. Harry leads us into other offices, introduces us. More smiles, more extended hands. Harry, host. We go into a corridor where a large video monitor hangs from the wall. Harry points down the corridor to the coffee, then disappears. A loudspeaker crackles: "Thirty minutes to detonation."

"Coffee?" Jim says.

"Sure. What do you think about this place?"

"Fascinating!"

We walk down to the coffee, pour some for ourselves, walk back to the monitor. The remote camera is fixed on a signpost out in the desert, probably over the point of detonation. I cannot read the sign.

"Better than a movie," Jim says. "But now we need a zoom."

Cactus, shrubs, saltbush or mesquite, and scrub grass. Perhaps there are beetles and bees and birds, out of camera range. An animal walks on, grazing on the scrub grass. Antelope. Then another, and another. The animals run off, and a pickup truck drives on. "Action," Jim says and smiles. The driver gets out and picks up what looks like a flag, drives off. Loudspeaker: "Fifteen minutes to detonation."

Harry reappears. "More coffee?"

"Not for me, thanks," says Jim. I smile and shake my head. People we have met come out of the offices, some carrying coffee cups. I catch familiar eyes, smile. Each takes a spot, a stand in front of the monitor. Cactus, shrubs, grass, and in the distance, a mountain. Five minutes. On the surface nothing moves. Underground, nothing. Four minutes, and now I think of how that voice is being carried over other speakers in other areas of the test site. Three minutes. Two minutes. One minute and counting. Thirty seconds. And then, whoomb! The floor moves, the earth, the earth trembles. Like ancient gods we make earth tremble. Dirt rises, rushes, storms. I hold my breath. Silence, total silence, as though no one dares breathe. We stare. What if, what if, what if . . . ? What if we have again created a radioactive cloud that will rise up from this Nevada desert and drift eastward and rain the slow, dreaded breast cancer upon the grandmothers and mothers and daughters of Utah?

Then the ground settles. Smiles, handshakes. Success. All power, poison, death stays in the earth.

But God said, What hast thou done?
The voice of thy brother's blood crieth
unto me from the ground.

We have been on the farm about as long as I worked in the weapon laboratories. If there is such a thing as karma, could I start paying off that karma now, by the shovelful? My shovel feels like a tool of hope, shoveling an act of faith. Some days. Other days, when the dogs come running through the orchard, or somebody out for a walk waves from the road, or a grosbeak lights on a branch and shows off his colors, I am not so sure I am paying off anything.

I REMEMBER years before cancer was even a part of my vocabulary hearing a writer read on the radio from her book about families. In their happiness, she said, all families were alike; it was in their suffering that they differed, that each suffered in its own way. We are all alone, we are each alone. But we do not want that. We are alone with our children who have cancer, with our own cancer of the spirit, and we do not want that.

We look for communion with fellow sufferers. We try to find rest and order. Instead, we find turbulence, we find chaos. Chaos is disorder. Turbulence is disorder at all levels and sizes. *Chaos* writer James Gleick describes turbulence as a condition of infinite modes, infinite movements, and infinite dimensions.

I used to think turbulence was about arroyo flooding, the clouds opening up over our hill and dumping all their moisture at once. If we are lucky Clovis or the mayordomo has already closed the acequia to minimize the flooding. But there is no time to call to find out—in fifteen minutes the arroyo begins to boil. I stand in the flow on the overshot shoveling out silt as fast as I can. If I reflect for one second I realize this is foolish; my shoveling has no effect at all, no effect on whether the flood goes over the boards and fills the acequia with silt, jumps out of the channel and tears up the road, dumps silt into the cider shed, the vineyards, all the irrigation laterals, no effect at all. But I do not reflect; I shovel faster and faster, like one possessed. Finally I jump out of the way. The torrent, the whole mesa in liquid form roars through the overshot, over the sides, half down the channel behind the tractor shed and the other half right down the road. I wave my arms, an officer, a runaway army. I think of Gayle standing on a rock on the storming Oregon coast, the breakers smashing around her, great white spouts thirty feet high, standing there, laughing, holding out her arms, conducting the performance of the Pacific. Then I drop my arms, shake my head. I am amazed, I am humbled. How can one small arroyo carry so much silt and so much water and run so fast? Turbulence.

And how can Marni, my daughter, pregnant with her first child, my grandchild-to-be, have cancer? I look everywhere for answers; nobody knows, nobody has any. Create your own. Art is our use of the energy of turbulence to create a new dynamic, a new tension, a new order. Or create a fear where none ever existed. And how can there not be something I can do to help heal her?

TODAY I walk down the road into the bright morning carrying a shovel, intent on water and geese and horses, and suddenly time breaks over me like a sneaker wave, sweeps me up in memory, and right in front of me I see that coyote dashing up the road to grab that gray goose. I shout, run down the road brandishing the shovel. The red dog tears out of the grapes, barking. The goose fights to get loose, all the geese honk, screech, howl. And at the very last moment, when I am just steps away, the coyote lets go and runs up the hill, followed by the red dog.

I close my eyes. I am in the orchard watching the water gushing from a dozen gopher holes. And there is the gopher, sitting on the edge of a hole, bewildered by the flood. Without a second for thought I smash it with my shovel. Instantly I am sorry, and I stare at the dead creature. The next time, and there is a next time, I chase off the barking dog, glove the blinking gopher no bigger than a softball, and carry it down to the safety of the riverbank.

The same farmer who bashes one gopher and rescues another snatches the canyon wren from the bobtailed cat, and traps one, two, three mice who were eating stored apples. The same farmer takes in one stranger with a rucksack, turns away another on a bicycle. He makes a promise, forgets, breaks a promise, keeps another, breaks another.

Both sides are balanced, and out of balance, the fair side up, the dark side up. I walk down the road saying

I will be aware today,
I will be aware today . . .

I miss a beat, trip, barely miss the ditch. My grandfather the wine maker was just my age when he died. His doctor had told him to give up the wine or he would die. He died anyway. Mother, too; died on the operating table at sixty-one when her heart didn't want to be fixed. All are dead now, grandparents, father, mother, godmother. I walk at the head of my line. My place is here, my time is this instant.

THESE ARE the parts of the farm today: the fields of boulders and the hills and mesas that border it on the south, and the river bordering it on the north, and the acequia that feeds it and the arroyo that slices into it, the sky, the clouds, the hens and their roosters, the guineas, the gray Toulouse geese, the brown duck and her two striped mallard offspring, the black alley cat and the gray and the seal-point Siamese, and, yes, the coyote that keeps watch over all the smaller animals that we let out of our sight for even an instant, and the red dog who is supposed to warn us of the coyote. And the farm is more than the sum of its parts.

The farm is more than the sum of its parts—I try to get hold of this. Like one rufous hummingbird sipping nectar is more than the sum of all that beating of wings? Like one woman lying naked in bed is a culmination of a million years of evolution? Maybe the farm is what's underneath the parts. I think what we do here is only a surface thing. The planting, cultivating, irrigating, harvesting, cider making, selling—that's just the top layer. And that's what we record, remember, share. The underneath is the work of others, magpies and sapsuckers, the sow bugs and the coddling moths, the honey bees and the paper wasps, and the black widows and the scorpions. Maybe the whole of it is an enormous bowl of sourdough, bubbling, fermenting, and ever rising.

THE FIRST doctor wants to grab the cancer, cut it out, do a mastectomy the next day.

No, my daughter says, no. Let's get a second opinion. Another examination. Worse news. A mastectomy won't do it; the cancer has spread to the lymphatic system. Now what? The baby is healthy. Radiation or chemotherapy could hurt the baby. Nontoxic treatments? Natural treatments? Mother or baby? Mother and baby? On the farm we run the scenarios. We ask questions. We have nothing to do with the decisions. But Marni feels we have.

"I'm in the middle," she tells Gayle. "If I go one way, my father will be unhappy and the other way my mother will be unhappy."

Forget that, forget us, I say. Do what you need to.

She decides. The baby is nonnegotiable. She will have the baby. And she will accept only treatments that will not harm the baby. As it turns out, a nurse in Denver has given low-dosage chemotherapy to a thousand pregnant women without harming the fetuses. Marni does chemo. And macrobiotic diet. And prayer. And Reiki healing. She literally changes her life.

In the eighth month she and Peter come up again. Rick, cider maker, obsidian knapper, spear-point spotter, and now sometime university music and anthropology student, is also here, with his new guitar. Marni and Peter have just seen the baby with ultrasonic scanning; it is healthy, beautiful. Marni shows her stomach, where the baby lives. She hides the pain in her side. She smiles, for herself and her baby. She has lost her hair, her thick, full long hair, but she radiates a peace and a love that makes me want to cry. Rick takes out his guitar and improvises for the child-to-be around the theme of "Blackbird." We listen, and maybe the baby listens. Perhaps this is how art transforms, releases the turbulence within, makes harmony out of chaos, makes the peace that passeth understanding.

WHEN THE cidermaster comes, I fear I still will not have completed the inventory of our orchards. I know I cannot keep in mind all the trees we have, which varieties they are, which have fruit ready to be picked, which must wait, which I have picked. So far I have tried to inventory the big orchard twice and reached only tree number 125. Then my mapping skills failed; I lost count, I couldn't read my own notes. In terms the aborigines might use, I was separated from the band, and I forgot the song of the orchard. I could say the gods and goddesses of the groves didn't want me there counting, so they sent winter crows and croaking magpies and canyon wrens, especially the canyon wrens, to distract me, but it wouldn't be true. I just never finished.

WANDA MILLET carries a notebook wherever she goes. I do not know how long she has been doing this, or whether she just started in the summer after Bill, her husband of forty-five years, passed away. Last Sunday Gayle was sitting next to her in the church choir. They had just finished hymn forty-nine. Wanda started writing again. "What are you writing?" Gayle asked.

"Just keeping the record," Wanda said. "See?"

"I can't read it."

"That's because it's shorthand. Here—'we sang hymn number 49. Gayle did a solo. It was good.'"

Andy McComb, the minister, announced the next hymn. The eleven members of the choir stood and sang along with the congregation. They finished and sat down, and Wanda wrote more. She says she is just keeping the record. She writes down just what happens. "Andy thanked us for coming. Choir practice is Monday at 7:30. Gayle took me home. She brought me Christmas cookies and dried apricots. I gave her that sparkling cider and chocolate chip cookies. . . ."

Wanda came here five years ago with her daughter and son-in-law and three grandchildren and her husband, Bill. Bill had suffered a stroke in Los Angeles, where he and Wanda had met and lived most of their lives. Then here in New Mexico, the promised land, he died. Pastor Andy noticed Wanda making notes during choir practice, and sometimes, when he forgot which hymns they had practiced for Sunday service, he would call her. Now, though Andy's calls have stopped, Wanda still keeps her record, still writes down what happens, holds on to life with her pen and her journal.

TREVOR KYLE Keegan is born in the middle of the cider season. Barbara Pepper, the minister who performed Marni and Peter's wedding at Alumni Chapel, is also the midwife who assists the birth at University Hospital. Peter and Susan are there. Later, Marni told me that despite her illness it was a perfect birth of a perfect baby.

Marni asks Gayle to come down to help bring Trevor home, to help care for him while she gets her strength back. Friends help. Peter takes Marni back into the hospital. Chemotherapy. The cancer does not go away. For all the chemotherapy the hospital can provide, the cancer does not go away, hardly backs off, but spreads.

I do not know what to do. I do not know what to say. I get up in the cold house, put the chore coat on over my pajamas, go outside, acknowledge dogs, cold, the sound of river, split one block, then another, load the box wood, pick up the wood box and the ash bucket and carry them inside, shovel the ashes out of the stove, set a large piece of wood in the back, crumple newspaper, lay on kindling and more wood, light the newspaper, open the damper, close the door, and watch. I watch the fire. Marni is fighting for her life. What does that mean?

I say to myself that I have lived a life. She is just beginning, with Trevor, with Peter, everything before her. I will swap. My health for her disease. I let go, she goes on. I watch. The fire takes hold. Why not? No way, no way, no way. And Marni is the last person in the world who would want to hear this crap.

TREVOR KYLE Keegan settled in with Marni and Peter, and Gayle came home.

"Trevor is fine," Gayle said. "Marni loves the baby. Peter loves the baby. But Marni is very tired. One night she got up while I was putting the baby down again after his feeding. 'I need a hug,' she said, and we stood there in the hall holding each other.

" 'It's so hard,' she said, 'to always be so tired. But I don't want to complain. I have everything I ever wanted. Someone to love and who loves me. A baby, a perfect baby. My own home. I have everything I dreamed of.'

"I said she might think of extending her dream. 'You might visualize having another child. And think of all the things you can do with Trevor, everything you want to teach him and show him. Maybe visualize the places you and Peter can take him. And the pleasure you will have watching him grow and being with him.'"

"And what did Marni say to that?" I asked.

"She listened, and she thanked me. 'I will have to think about it.' But she was very tired."

I listened, I wanted to hear everything. Marni could say things to Gayle and Gayle could say things to Marni that would never be said between Marni and me.

THROUGHOUT THE winter, Marni's treatment regimen shaped her days and our days. Hands-on healing, supplements, pure diet, Chinese herbs, massage, meditation, manipulation, and the ever present chemicals dripping into her bloodstream to kill the cancer. Have faith, believe, visualize, say prayers, and put out of your head all those doubts and fears and prejudices. We watched videos on healing, listened to tapes on healing, read books on healing, talked with friends who had been healed or who had other friends in the process. I tried to put out of my mind and heart everything but the thought that Marni would be healed, nothing about the madness of a treatment that put her in the hospital, that tore apart the very body struggling to heal itself.

In the spring Marni took a break from treatment, and she and Peter and Trevor flew to Pittsburgh and Boston to visit Peter's family and friends, and just to get away. They brought back pictures. The three of them in the park, in the sunshine, the spires of Pittsburgh behind them, smiling, the long hair that almost looked like Marni's own hair. They came home. More tests, more treatment.

MARCH 1995. But I am thinking of the March that Trevor was five months old. I am working in a small adobe building on the upper bank of the acequia. I look out the small window over the desk. A field of boulders rises before me. Above are more boulders come to rest on the slope, boulders all the way up to the one perched on a great rock against the sky. Out the glass door and out the west window I see more boulders on other slopes, behind the garage, behind the house. Some are camouflaged, by piñons and junipers, by sage and chamisa. But I know they are there. These boulders are basalt, the remains and reminders of the Valle Grande eruptions. I remember reading how long ago that was, but I do not remember the number. Yet even if I looked it up, I would still not know how long it took the lava to crack, the rivers to erode the hills, and the boulders to roll down to where they now lie. Or when the boulders will roll again.

Everything that ever happened is still happening. The boulders. Some crumble. They become the rocks for the walls of our house. Some do not. The rock wall of the old chicken house is built upon a boulder too big to move. Neighbor Michael Valdez told me his method for dealing with a boulder too big to move: dig a hole next to it, then push it in and bury it. But I could not begin to bury all the boulders on the hills above us.

That one or another boulder may someday tumble down upon us is nothing we have control of. Everything is still happening. The worst case, a few years ago, was the boulder as big as a smokehouse that bounced down on the Taos highway and took off the front of a bus and killed four people.

Everything that ever happened. Father Meyers planting the trees in the orchard. The settlers with picks and shovels and bare hands moving the rocks and cutting the acequia into the steep slope of the hill. The Pueblo people hunting here before the acequia. And the people before the Pueblo people. And the deer and the coyote and the bear and the cougar before any people. And before the earth, before the sun, before the stars. Everything that ever happened is still happening.

Out the west window is the house and behind and above it junipers and sage and piñon and more boulders. The trees and rocks and boulders go all the way up to the peak, to our television antenna and the unpainted wooden cross next to it.

4 A.M. I wake with a feeling of loss. My first son, my oldest, is forty today. So much has happened. So much has been forgotten. I do not know what I can do, or want to do. I step out into the night. Snow is everywhere. It blankets the acequia, the bridge, the road, the garden, the fields. It cloaks the willows, the lilacs, the roses, the plums, the peaches, the apricots, the apples. Everything is covered, everything is lost.

Not so. Nothing is lost. The river fills the darkness, fills the night with its old voice, its voice far older than I or those half-mythical people who inhabited this house before us, who planted the fruit trees, carried the earth in barrows to fill the terraces, carried the rocks off the hillside to make the walls. Nothing is lost.

I stand here on the porch, under the stars. The cold breaks through the cloak of house-warmth, bed-warmth, moves under the flannel pajamas, right up to my skin. My chest tightens. But I stand here, listening.

Nothing is lost. The river speaks. It speaks for the passing waters, the gravel and sand underneath, the boulders, the roots of cottonwoods and willows and New Mexico olives and grasses reaching out from the banks. It speaks for all the works men and beavers have put into her bed—the bridge pilings, the riprap and woven-brush dams and earthen and rock headings for the acequias. It speaks also for the coyotes and rabbits and bears and deer and the Anasazi hunters and every creature who came down to drink at dusk or in the early morning, and for the trout and suckers and water snakes and monsters of our dreams who live in the river. Nothing is lost, no footfall, no fruit, no blossom, no leaf, not even the smallest grain of pollen, fallen into the stream. Everything is remembered, every splash, every thought, every drop of water, and every drop of blood.

IT IS a warm Easter afternoon, and fishermen and families and young people have set themselves up all along the banks of the river. Fishermen in hip boots are casting into the thigh-deep waters, and others are casting from rocks along the shore. Women are sitting on blankets and in chairs next to red and blue picnic chests. Young people lean against their cars, holding their twelve- and sixteen-ounce aluminum cans.

Just across the bridge we turn. The road follows the river upstream in a series of humps and dips. Rocks bang against the oil pan, the gas tank, the springs and struts. At the first turnout we stop. We lock the picnic chest in the car and carry our gear up the road—Jamie, his fishing rods; Gayle, her painting water; Rick, the red canteen; and I, the yellow pack with extra clothes and Gayle's watercolor pad and paints.

Five hundred years ago we might have been a band of hunters from the Pueblo, stalking deer. Three hundred years ago we might have been Spanish explorers, hoping that this path did not lead to yet another box canyon in this godforsaken country. And four thousand years ago we might have been nomadic hunters, the Anasazi, the people who came before. It is hard to believe that no footprint we make on this land is a first, that every resting place we find has been found before. How can that possibly be in such a vastness?

We pass a pickup parked against the hill; it could belong to any of the fishermen on this bank or the other. Jamie peels off with his rod and tackle box full of handmade flies.

Ahead of us, just before the gorge begins, mesas, mountains, water, sky—everything comes together. Gayle stops. She sees what she wants to paint. Rick goes on. I leave the pack with her and follow him.

The road turns into a path. Rick is already hunting, poking his way through the sagebrush at the edge of the road. I'm poking my eyes into the rapids. Rick stops. End of the road, end of the path. La junta del Rio Grande y del Rio de Taos. The Taos courses out of a side canyon, the one that carries the state road off the mesa. Swollen by the early runoff it splashes mightily, pretending to be a real river. The closer it comes to its end, the more boisterous it becomes, ending now in a white finale over the great boulders and into the Rio Grande. I finger each falling column, follow the line of foam, the flash, white. A confluence, a coming together.

But the Rio Grande, even at its summer driest, remains our fifth-longest river; no one expects it to fuss because of the Taos. Now, at the beginning of spring runoff, with whole mountains of snow behind it, the Rio Grande accepts the waters of the Rio Taos with barely a flicker of recognition and moves on.

Rick says he has been here before, with a friend. Now he wants to climb up to the first level, just to see what turns up. We all want to find something, we are always looking for something. I follow, then look back at the confluence. And we are always leaving something behind.

Last fall we were walking in the first range of hills above the farm, about halfway between the Rio Oscuro below us and the lava caves just beyond the rim of the mesa, and Rick found a four thousand–year-old projectile point. This kind of thing happens so often I have accused him of carrying discoveries in his pocket, then "finding them" just to irk me. He laughs at that; "Of course, that's exactly what I do."

This point was half buried in the silt, under a small juniper. Only the fins were showing. It did not look like any of the other points he had found on these mesas. Those are mostly obsidian, and with or without tips their edges are usually jagged, still sharp enough to cut after five hundred years and more of exposure. But the edges and fins of this one were rounded, worn smooth, and it was not obsidian but basalt. He had not seen one like this before.

At the Maxwell Museum of Anthropology a curator identified the point as Rio Grande, the product of Anasazi hunters who predated the modern Pueblos.

Did that Anasazi hunter carry this point on an arrow, and did he let it fly from his bow? Or was it on a spear? And what animal? Would it stop a deer? Could he hit a rabbit? Or was it for a human, someone from another band? Rick let me hold the point, and I tried to understand the voice. I know the point has this record in itself. But how to read it, or interpret it if the script is shorthand? It is not easy, I think, but it is possible.

All time is here, all ages live, nothing is lost. The animals that used to be, the river passing, the flow of the all. But the problem is how to hold on to even our own memories, our truths, our experiences and then make meaning out of them. Edna Millay wrote sixty years ago that the mark of our age was the unceasing "meteoric shower of facts." Now it has become a deluge, and we struggle to hold on to branches, rocks, anything to keep from drowning.

I think of Wanda Millet who keeps her own record, as long as she can write, whether or not she or anyone will ever use it, because that is her way.

" 'DRINK-YOUR-tea, drink-your-tea,' that's his call," our friend Julia says.

"And there he is," says Monte, her husband, and he points to the tip of an ironwood bush at the edge of the mesa, right over the acequia.

I fix the bird in the glasses—black head, white belly, sides robin-red, rows of white spots on his dark wings, a blade of song against the sky: rufous-sided towhee. "Drink-your-tea," he calls to the ditch, the orchard, the river. "Drink-your-tea, drink-your-tea." It's the end of April, early morning. We stand just below the house, by the bridge over the acequia. The acequia is flowing again after the long winter. Down the road the orchard swims in pink and white blossoms. And above us the just-greening willows are alive with birds.

Monte and Julia have come from Santa Fe to bird the farm. They know our land well. Julia and Gayle have painted together: our ducks and geese and dogs and the Ford 8N tractor that re-fuses to die, the old Dodge stake-bed truck that has died and is awaiting resurrection, and the outbuildings and sheds at various stages of decline and resuscitation. The four of us have walked to the confluence of our river with the Rio Grande, and we have climbed to the cave on La Mesita a thousand feet above us. Monte and I have dug holes for planting trees. And we have cleaned ditches together.

The world is filled with the Absolute, according to Teilhard de Chardin and Annie Dillard, and "to see this is to be made free." For Monte and Julia the good world is absolutely filled with birds. They are heralds of hope, deities of delight. They are free-dom. And on this small farm between the rock and juniper hill-side and the bosque and the river, the birds are everywhere. Appleland? Birdland.

Down the road we head with glasses and field guides, stopping at every whoop and rustle. Before we reach the end of the farm we have twelve species:

junco
white-crowned sparrow
robin
starling

ash-throated flycatcher
yellow-rumped warbler
Wilson's warbler
pine siskin
scrub jay
hairy woodpecker
flicker
rufous-sided towhee

"That's a lot for ten acres," Monte said. "What's special about your farm is being between the mesa with its juniper-sage habitat and the river."

"And there's the acequia," I said. "More water right at the edge of the dry land."

"Yes."

"And I hope the songbirds appreciate our benign neglect of the pruning saw and the absence of the sprayer."

He smiled. "I'm sure they do, my friend."

But besides our benign habitat, Monte said that feed was a big attraction for the birds: the dry, datelike fruit of the Russian olive, the hips of the wild roses, the purple berries of Virginia creeper, the apples, pears, peaches, plums, apricots, mulberries, and grapes, plus all the worms and insects.

At other times and in other seasons on the farm Julia and Monte have found other birds. Lewis's woodpecker, which catches insects in the air like a flycatcher, likes to sit on the bare, dead limbs at the top of the Lombardy poplars along the road in the early-morning sun, as if displaying its iridescent green back and plum-red belly. The western wood peewee also catches insects on the wing from its bare treetop perch. The ouzel, also known as the American dipper, perches on rocks in the river, watching and waiting, then launches like a gray bullet, skimming just above the water until it bores into the river, as easily and naturally as it flies, to feed on underwater insects and small fish. Canyon wrens, whose long falling trill is like no other birdcall, love the basaltic boulders above the old hog pen. When Monte approaches they call "jeet, jeet, jeet, jeet," and bob in and out of crevices. And we see blue grosbeaks and house finches and barn swallows, and hawks and turkey vultures soaring overhead. Once just over our heads a Cooper's hawk dove out of the sky to take a ruby-crowned kinglet taking off from the big willow, and missed. Or at least that's what Monte told us had happened; all I could see was the flash of wings and the rustle of the branches. And in the summer we have the hummingbirds.

WE FIRST met Karen Hayes at Marni and Peter's. Dr. Hayes was an assistant professor of developmental psychology at the University of New Mexico. She was from North Carolina. Though she was only a few years older than Marni, Professor Hayes had been Marni's thesis advisor. That spring Karen resigned her position at the University. She planned to start a school for preschool children that would combine nurturing and teaching. She wanted to design a playroom-classroom environment that would be an integral part of the learning-nurturing process. And she wanted Marni to teach in her new school.

Marni and Karen spent hours talking about the school. Marni wanted to work with Karen. But first Marni needed to get well. Karen asked how she could help. Come take care of Trevor, Marni had said. And Karen had agreed.

When the spring semester ended, Karen began her new school with one student, eight-month-old Trevor Kyle Keegan. She came each weekday morning at eight as Peter was leaving for work. She taught Trevor. And more. She took care of Trevor and Marni, and she did whatever had to be done around the house.

Marni's chemotherapy had been going on for almost a year. She would finish one course, rest, then start another. And she continued the other treatments, the Reiki, the diet, the meditation. Karen's presence brought a calm, a grounding to the household; whatever Marni needed to do she could do without worrying about Trevor or the house. And whenever Marni wanted to see or hold her son, her perfect baby, Trevor was right in the next room.

Karen brought other kinds of blessings to me. I could ask her what was happening to my daughter, and she would tell me, kindly, but straight: Marni wasn't getting worse, but she wasn't getting better. And that was a truth I did not want to face. From the very beginning of Marni's illness I had pledged to myself that whatever treatments she and Peter decided upon and undertook, I would support completely and never, under any circumstances, would I raise any questions. And I had kept that pledge. At the same time what she was going through was tearing me apart because I doubted its value at the deepest level of my being, and not only doubted its value, but thought it was doing her harm. Not the Reiki, not the meditation, not the hands-on healing, not the diet, but the chemotherapy. I believed the doctors administering the treatment meant well, that they were doing everything they knew to heal Marni. But I doubted that they really understood the consequences of administering to a sensitive body and spirit the gross form of treatment I believed chemotherapy to be. I talked to no one except Gayle about my doubts; that was part of my pledge of support. At the same time I struggled with them. I hoped I was wrong, that chemotherapy would work.

I would walk through the orchard among the trees upon which I would never think of administering any kind of poison. The bees, the whole insect world and their wildflower hosts, and the birds, all that lived together in the orchard I protected as best I could. And my daughter, on chemotherapy—it seemed insane. Surely there were herbs here that could be made into potions that could help her. If only I knew what they were and how to work with them. No, no. First of all I did not know, and, second, even if I thought I knew what might help, I had pledged, pledged silence. And at the same time I wanted my doubts to be wrong, I prayed that they were wrong; to overcome my doubt I sowed faith within myself in every way I could. There is only so much a father can do to make things turn out right for his daughter. Trying to understand was what I could do.

I thanked Karen, for being there for Marni.

She looked at me. "Marni is one of mine," she said, "and I was brought up to take care of what is mine."

"And you, you're part of my family," I said.

MIDDLE OF June, first day of the Santa Fe Farmers' Market. Friday evening we picked mulberries, the only fruit ripe. Saturday morning I left at quarter to six, before light, and pulled into space number 7 at quarter to seven. Rose Mary and Stan Crawford were already setting out their greens and garlic and bouquets in number 6.

"Harvey!" Rose Mary called in that rich voice of her Australian homeland. "I'm glad you're here!" I got out, she came over, we hugged. "And how's Marni?"

"She's not getting worse," I said. "But she's not getting better."

Rose Mary looked at me. "It's awful, just awful."

Awful. Yes. Then what was I doing, coming to market as if this were just another summer in our lives, this week mulberries, then plums, then apricots, then peaches and pears and apples and cider?

"And how is Peter, and little Trevor?" Dear Rose Mary, full of caring, the Santa Fe Farmers' Market, and no place to cry.

END OF June, another New Mexico Arts Fair, the State Fairgrounds in Albuquerque. I cleaned out the farm truck. It took most of the day to load: Gayle's watercolor paintings, bubble-wrapped half sheets and quarter sheets in one large wooden box and several cardboard boxes and full sheets in their individual boxes; pegboard and cloth and lights, and the tools and screws to put the booth together; a small dry sink that had belonged to Gayle's grandmother that Gayle had rescued from the cellar and covered with Mexican tile; a bridge table and folding chairs and a rug to cover asphalt; and, squeezed in at the last, two pots of geraniums and a water bucket of fresh-cut lilies. Then we found yet more space for our suitcases.

Saturday afternoon. And amidst the hundreds upon hundreds

sauntering by the booths, looking and some buying, there was Marni, smiling, so thin but smiling, in her wig, taking Trevor in his stroller to his first arts and crafts fair. And Peter and Karen and Sam. I watched Marni looking at Gayle's paintings, the flowers, the landscapes, as she had done many times, at many fairs, even sat the booth for us.

Then we sat on the grass across from the booth. Marni asked how the fair was, how we were doing. The sales were good. Had she walked around, what did she think of the fair? She smiled, we talked about the things she liked, the people, normal things. It was good to see Karen here, and Peter with old friend Sam without whom there would have been no Marni and Peter and Trevor. Then Marni called Peter, and we came back to reality. "I'm getting tired, dear. I want to go home now."

Two weeks later I talked to Peter; what might we do to honor our shared birthday on the first of August? He and Marni had a plan. Mark and Jacque and Corin were coming down from Denver; they would come up from Albuquerque with Trevor. Everyone would meet at the farm, then they would do an overnight camp in mountains. Could Marni do that? She wanted to, for his birthday, Peter said. And how was the chemo doing? Discontinued, he said. It wasn't doing any good.

The next week Susan's friend Jim, the metal sculptor, stopped by. He had just come from Albuquerque. His face was flushed, and he seemed more intense than I remembered him. We asked him in.

"I don't have time, I'm meeting someone in Taos. But Susan asked me to stop."

We sat down on the front porch where we had all sat so many times, looking at the flowers, the water flowing in the acequia, the clouds.

"Have you talked to Susan?"

"No. What's going on?"

"When are you going down to Albuquerque to see Marni?"

"Marni and Peter are coming up on the first, in two weeks, for Peter's birthday."

"If I were you," he said, "I would go down now."

"What's happened? We haven't heard anything."

"I've been there a couple of days, with Susan."

"How is Marni?"

He didn't answer, or if he did answer I didn't hear what he said because his look was so intense, like the flame from his welding torch, scorching. Then he said, "Susan wants you to come down. That's what she told me, and that's what I'm telling you."

He accepted a drink of water, and he left.

I called Marni's house, and Susan answered. How was Marni? She was resting. I told Susan what Jim had said, that we should come right down. She seemed surprised; she hadn't said that. Had Marni gotten worse, then? She was having pain in her liver, but not any worse than before. Were they still planning to come up on the first? Yes, as far as she knew. I told Susan I did not know what to do. Gayle and I could drive down now, I said; we could get someone to take care of the animals. What did she think? And under that question was another: how could I ask Susan what I, her father, should do about her sister so determined to live and the cancer so determined she should not?

MANY TIMES, especially on warm days, I have turned around in the chicken pen because I definitely heard someone talking, only to find there was no one, only the soft sounds of the Araucanas and the Buff Orpingtons, pecking in the dirt and just being with each other. More than once the sounds were so human, people murmuring, speaking quietly, talking to each other and to themselves, that there had to be someone in the pen, if not a living person, then a spirit person. I never caught a sentence or phrase, or even a word I could recognize. If I had, then I might have to listen for words in the guineas murmuring in the mulberry at night, a murmur more mellow than water rippling, leaves fluttering. Or listen for meaning in the humming strumming of the crickets, the undersound of our firmament. I do not know if I'm ready for that now. Someday, perhaps, when the voices inside become quiet.

PART 4

Walking the Orchard

First Irrigation
A splotch of yellow in the new ditch—
the old moon sneaks into the garden.

SOMEONE ASKED ME once how he could learn what apple growing is about. I said one way to learn is by walking. Walking through the orchard, day after day. Looking at the trees. Cutting out the deadwood. Pruning. Looking. Pruning. Hauling away the wood. Walking through the snow. Walking through the rain. The wind. The mud. Under the sun, under the clouds, in the rain. Watching the blossoms. Putting in the water. Opening gates. Closing gates. Trenching, ditching. Watching the water. Listening to the weather. Watching the thermometer. After the overnight frost picking the green pip, breaking it open, carefully, trying to be objective, aloof, apart, scientific. Then looking inside. Green? Or black? And then again. Another tree, another week. Green? Black?

Walking through the orchard, watching the trees, watching the apples. One day Rick comes up from Albuquerque to visit, and he walks through the orchard. "Are you going to have fruit this year!" he says. And around the mesa, just a mile up the road in the orchards of the village, nothing. Not one apple in a dozen trees. Whole orchards with maybe a half box, maybe nothing at all.

ON OUR hands and knees the plot thickens to a green maze through which our fingers finesse the sandbur grass, the false tomatilla, the white clover and yellow clover, the alfalfa, fledgling sunflowers and bee balm–cum-milkweed, and the myriad stout and stunted stems, finesse them out ever so gently, but out. And if they refuse reason, if they resist my fingers or John's, if they fiercely clutch the meat and bones of the soil, still they must come out, screaming, pulling great clumps of soil with their roots. However they wish, our purpose is inexorable.

Behind us the new raspberry shoots stand demurely in the naked soil, not yet sure how they should take this sudden release from confinement. "Now that looks like we've accomplished something," John says. I agree, though I'm not sure exactly what.

John Veltman, my friend and helper-for-the-day, John the mathematician, John the inventor, is not a farmer. Last year he retired from the San Antonio Public Schools and moved with his wife to northern New Mexico, "because this is where we always wanted to live." I met him at a men's gathering. Today he is taking a day off from his inventing to loan us his hands. He sits back like a Buddha with heels planted atop the furrow and bends forward over his crossed legs to pull and toss, pull and toss, an endless chant of the farmer in his field. "Did I tell you about the fat calculator?"

He describes his latest invention. A shopper takes it with her into the store and dials in the total calories per serving and the calories of fat shown on the product label. The calculator then shows the actual percentage of fat that will be consumed by eating the product.

"These are the numbers used by dieticians and doctors," he says. "A feta cheese label, for example, might read 12 percent fat, but that's based on weight. The actual fat as a percentage of calories might be 78 percent."

I listen and I am impressed. John has invented educational tools for teaching mathematics that are now used around the country. I like having John here working with me this July morning, for what his hands do, for the ideas he shares, and for the ideas they evoke in me.

Order (infinite repetition of form)
    the fern, each branch a replica of the whole
    Bach
Chaos (infinite repetition of disorder, randomness)
    capitalism, the "success" of chaos
Fractal (tool for measuring infinite change, John Veltman)
    coastline
    brain surface
    evolution
    marriage
Order versus Chaos
    weeding the raspberries
    working a marriage
    performing Beethoven's violin concerto
    pruning
Creative Process
    painting Guernica
    planting
    writing the violin concerto
    nuclear testing and fallout
    cancer, the creation we fear
Patriarchy
    empire building
    "Thy will be done"
    "For your own good" (Alice Miller)
Unpredictability
    late frost
    arroyo flooding
    Marni's cancer

PICKING THE first apples. This year las Manzanas de Julio come in June. August apples in July. September apples in August. By the second week of August we are picking, and we press out the first juice by the fifteenth. Not the sour juice of the crab apple I have used in leaner years, juice that turns before I can get it to market. But real cider. A little light, but real cider.

And we pick, and pick. Without picking apples, how can you make cider? Other years we have bought unsprayed apples, but this year nobody has any. So we pick even the trees with just handfuls of fruit. The early trees first, in the west end of the orchard. By the road. Between the road and the pump house.

Walking through the orchard now I have to decide where to pick each day, what to do tomorrow and next week. I taste. I bite into fruit that is green by design, the Yellow Transparent. They go first. I taste the very earliest reds, lightweight fruit, though from their redness and size they could be mistaken for their late-season cousins. They are softer than the fall fruit even at their firmest, and thin-flavored. But they are still apples, real apples, not crabs, not plastic. I taste one or two from each of the half-dozen trees in this row, in the far northeastern corner, across the road from the river, just inside our fence. These we will mix with the Yellow Transparents and what is left of the Manzanas de Julio.

I talk with James, Gayle's youngest, recently out of the Navy and helping us this season. I walk with him into the orchard and point to a particular tree across from the pump house. "Please start there," I say, "that tree with all the apples."

"Which one?"

"There is only one," I say. "Look." Jamie looks, shakes his head. And suddenly I remember; he is color-blind. "I'm sorry," I say, and we walk right up to the tree.

"Oh," he says, "this one."

"I guess you can see it better close up."

"Yes, but it has nothing to do with color," he says. "Apples and leaves have different sizes and different shapes." We do this first picking together, as we will do many more pickings together. Then Joshua appears, and he picks with James.

We stack the filled boxes in the cider shed. We separate the stacks, marking each so we can tell without taking off the tops. Now we are ready.

Our rack-and-cloth cider press dictates the cider-making process. Grind apples into pomace. Set the first rack in the juice tray, drape a cloth over the rack, and set the square form on top. Pour a heaping bucket of pomace into the form, smooth it, remove the form, and fold the cloth into a pillow. Set the next rack on top of the pillow and repeat the process, thus building our tower of pomace-filled racks. Then grind more, build higher, until we reach the top.

When the three of us are working together, James and I work on the stack while Josh works the grinder. James stands on one side of the press, and I stand on the other. I bucket the pomace into the form, and James smoothes it out. I remove the form, and we fold the cloth together. His folds are always clean, neat, much neater than mine. He has a knack for working with food going back to his three-year stint as a cook in the Navy. One day we were making something in the kitchen, and he showed me how to mince an onion. First cut it in half, then make close longitude cuts across the hemisphere. Then across the latitudes. It's the one cutting job I do reasonably well now, thanks to James.

Within the cidering process we sometimes fine-tune the flavor. After grinding perhaps three boxes of tart and two of sweet and building a stack eight racks high, we taste the juice that has dripped into the barrel, and then consult on what the final box of that pressing should be. But usually we have a pretty good idea how the juice will turn out, and we taste only the total pressing before bottling. In the middle of the season our orchard offers many varieties for blending. At the end, we almost always have an abundance of Red Delicious, and we must stretch the tarts to keep the juice from getting too sweet. In a good cider year the Romes and Winesaps hold out till the end of October. Other years we may have to stop making cider and just take the late Red Delicious to market.

When all ten racks are stacked with pomace, we lock the press and start pumping the jack. The great cider gurgle begins. The press becomes a fountain of cider, raining juice from every level, every side, every surface, every inch of fabric, down into the collector, then down the pipe into the barrel. When the fountain slackens we pump the stack higher, tighter, then watch and listen, hoping that gurgling of the golden liquid surging down the pipe will not stop until the barrel is full. Toward the end of the flow we tilt the whole press forward, then backward, then balance it on one corner to get every last drop of juice from the pressing.

Now we load bottles into the filling tray. In theory we can put our cider in any size bottle available, half-pints, pints, quarts, half-gallons, and gallons. In the first year we used only gallons. Then grocery stores asked for half-gallons. We added half-gallons. Later, other local cider makers began selling to the same stores and added quarts and pints and even half-pints. This gave them more shelf space and an entry into the single-drink market. With some misgiving, we tried the smaller sizes. Filling the smaller sizes took more time, but the range of sizes looked good on cooler shelves. The tall pints felt good in the hand. They sold well, even with the higher per-ounce container cost. Yet I didn't feel good about using all that throwaway plastic. We went back to gallons and half-gallons. And this year we standardized on half-gallons.

As we load the filling tray I muse about the old days, and I talk about maybe using gallons again. For one thing, they are easier to fill. They also use less material. Josh says no. He puts his face right up to mine.

"Follow your resolve. Ours is special. No sprays. Handpicked apples, nothing off the ground. This is sipping cider, right? We don't sell to guzzlers, right?"

I laugh. This nephew is a true believer. I will mark that in the book for the cidermaster.

IF THERE were some way of knowing precisely or even approximately when a messenger was coming, we might be on the lookout, and we might be more open to investigating various forms and shapes and habits. We might be more likely to suspend our usual judgments and skepticism. We might even see a strange form as a guise or disguise, and look at it before rejecting it. And if we had time enough, in advance, we might even look inside ourselves, look at our barricades, our hair-trigger defenses, and decide if they were the proper way, the way we would want to welcome the messenger, the teacher.

But we do not know in advance, and there is no way to know. The carrier, the bringer comes always in his own time, in her own size, in its own skin.

Two years ago a thin-faced, graying man pedaled up our road on a rusty one-speed bicycle. I saw a newspaper rolled up in the pocket of his worn suit jacket. I saw the number 5 with two o's after it written with a magic marker on the sides of his tennis shoes. I read Goodwill. I read cheap wine. I read all-night café, hands nursing a cup of coffee, eyes aimed blankly at a newspaper.

The dogs barked and ran toward him. I called them and I told him not to worry, they were friendly. I walked over. What could I do for him, I asked. Someone on the highway said "the German" had apples to pick. Was this the place? The German? Well, that was one way of distinguishing Frauenglass from Romero. I thanked him for asking. But this year we didn't have a lot of apples, and I was doing the picking myself.

"That's all right," he said. "I'm just asking." He petted the big dog. There was a Great Dane just like ours on a ranch he had worked on in Wyoming. Good with the animals, but it wanted to be inside at night. I listened. It was getting dark, and I wanted to get on with loading the truck. I said I had to get going.

"I understand," he said. "That's all right." He pedaled down the road. But as soon as he was out of sight I realized I had done the wrong thing. I ran up to the house. I told Gayle I'd just made a mistake. I jumped in the car and drove after him. I had to find this man, to bring him back, to share supper with him, at least. I could find some picking for him, on Sunday, and next week. Of course! I would fix it. I did not see him on the road to Rio Oscuro. I turned back, and sped down the highway toward Velarde. No. Then I drove north, upriver toward Taos. No. He was nowhere.

It was almost dark, but I went back to the tree to finish picking the bushel I had started. How could he just disappear? Of course, I knew that question was irrelevant. I had judged the man and turned him away. I could not fix that.

AS MARNI fought the cancer with all her consciousness and spiritual strength, a network of friendship wove around her and offered baby-sitting, errand running, driving, and then food, healing food for Marni and her family. Graduate students in the University of New Mexico Psychology Department, people with whom she had shared offices, taken classes, worked on research projects, danced, partied, or just talked, along with other longtime friends and new friends—a network, a system, a guild of honorable cooks prepared meals and made sure that every weeknight someone dropped off a meal, a different one each night, and always with the foods Marni liked and could eat. The deliverers stayed barely long enough to ask how she was doing, to see if there was something else they could do, to give hugs, and then be off. When I visited there was always a stack of washed serving dishes by the door ready to be picked up.

I had seen a similar network develop in our village, for a single mother who almost lost her leg in an auto accident, for a woman who came back from Egypt with hepatitis, for another with a brain injury. Now my daughter was at the nexus of this caring. With daily kindnesses, her friends were now entering themselves in the great book of selfless acts, the book without beginning and without end.

AT FIRST I'm careful. I step around the holes, over the deepest runs of the current. I suspect Clovis is doing the same thing. We both have the same knee-high irrigation boots. They're fine for getting around in flooded fields. The river, even in summer at its lowest flow, is another matter. Our careful stepping around and over the deeper parts is ultimately useless—and we know it. We're just pretending we're not going to get wet.

Such niceties are lost on Dan; he's wearing regular work shoes. There's nowhere he could step without getting wet. But boots or no boots, we're happy to see him. Two more hands to build the weir.

Here the Rio Oscuro is maybe forty feet wide. Our weir will run twenty-five or thirty feet, from the far bank to the beginning of our channel. We're here because this week the river dropped, silt has built up in the channel, and we're not getting nearly enough flow into the acequia. I watch Clovis set the height. His piles are three or four rocks high. I match him. Then he steps out from the main piling maybe ten feet and drops one large rock and then another: a cairn in the rio to mark the water's way. He heads toward a log thrown up on the breakwater. I step into a hole. The cool July waters of the Rio Oscuro pour into my boots, soak my feet and legs. We bend into the water. I take hold of a large, flat rock slick with algae and tufted with water weed and then another and another. I stack them. It becomes a column, a three-layer job. Then we start another column, six or eight feet upstream. These two columns will hold a log.

I remember now having this feeling of stepping into a hole deeper than my boots before. I have lived it, dreamed about it: the next morning awake in the marriage bed with a stranger and a promise. Every step brings differences of depth and differences in temperature and current. Every step is uncertain, but you keep walking.

The rocks are smooth, hard to get hold of. Never mind. Find the big ones. Use the shovel to loosen what the flow has buried. Carry it to the weir. Up, splash. One rock at a time. The water gets deeper above our little dam. We don't talk. Clovis goes after a great stone at the very edge of the channel. He levers his shovel under it, feels a shift. Now he bends into the water. He has the muscled shoulders and arms of a lifetime of farming and working on the acequia. I bend beside him. We pull together. The stone rolls out of its hole. We tumble it over and over. Dan waits at the bank. He has pushed aside smaller rocks. We aim for the space he has made. Now all three of us in the water, under, above, in front of the stone, which becomes bigger as it surfaces. We heave it into place. All right.

Now the water begins to work for us. It washes around the hole. It picks up silt and pebbles and carries them away, deepening our channel.

ROBERT FROST wrote a poem called "After Apple Picking" in which he speaks of having picked so many apples he still feels the rungs of the picking ladder on his feet and the apples in his hands and dreams there is no end to apples. I understand what it is to be tired like that after the harvest, after pressing the thousandth gallon of cider. But I am no poet. In between the end of one season and the beginning of another I muse about the process in a more prosaic way: I make a list.

Eleven Skills a Cidermaster Must Have
1. Knowing the taste of his own cider
2. Judging ripeness
3. Blending the flavors of his apples
4. Picking consciously and harmoniously
5. Deciding when to pick
6. Deciding which to pick first
7. Picking at the right time of each day
8. Deadwooding his trees
9. Pruning his trees
10. Singing to his trees
11. Listening to his trees

WHAT KIND of a person was Friedrich Meyers, orchardist, vintner, educator, former pastor of San Ysidro? It depends upon whom you ask. All of the old-timers in the village knew him, whether they attended San Ysidro or the Oscuro Presbyterian Mission Church. And each has his own opinion.

"He was a hard man."

"He was a generous man."

"He made my grandmother tithe him a pig every spring even though she was barely surviving, raising the family after her husband died. I never liked him."

"He believed in education."

"He pulled our family pew out of the church and set it on the front steps the first Sunday after my father took my two older brothers out of his Catholic school and put them into the Presbyterian school. But Father Meyers didn't hold a grudge. When I came around looking for a job picking fruit, he hired me."

According to a recent story in a weekly newspaper, Father Meyers was a man who made things happen. Families in the village still talk about the "aggressive" priest from Germany. Before he came there were only county-run elementary schools. There was no money to build a high school in the northern valleys. Meyers went back east to get donations. Money came from as far away as New York. He brought in teachers from a midwestern religious order who were better educated than the local teachers. Father Meyers, as one man put it, gave the people in these small villages a chance to become something.

Some in the village might wonder why I go to so much trouble to balance these accounts about Father Meyers. I feel it is important to be accurate, but some might feel my interest is more personal than I am admitting. Olaf, my first orchard helper, asked me outright one day when I was taking him home from picking apples: "Are you Father Meyers's son?"

"No, Olaf. Where did you get that idea?"

"I don't know. I just wondered," he said.

Corina denied to her dying breath that there was any son or any hidden relationship between Victoria and Father Meyers. She did not convince the neighbors. Then, two years ago during the annual art tour, a woman who grew up in the village took me aside, to set the record straight, she said. Not only did Father Meyers and Victoria have a son, but he was adopted by her relatives, he was now living in southern Colorado, and she would bring him to meet us the next week. She did not return that week. This year I saw her again at the open house.

"Do you remember your promise?" I asked her.

"Yes, I remember," she said. "I asked him. I told him I would come here with him. But he refused. He wasn't interested."

I have thought of that alleged son of Victoria and Friedrich more than once, and of his mother and father. I try to imagine what it would be like to have a child and let go of that child forever. I wonder if they ever talked about him. I do not understand how it would be possible to not do so, to not even mention his name to one another.

MANY COME to help in making cider. There are the regulars who come every week. There are the annuals, those who helped last year and come back especially to do it again. And there are the children and grandchildren. Of course, we have also had help in every season, with fruit picking and planting, and every kind of repair and improvement project. And we have not lacked for guests or return visits from those bringing their own friends and guests. The farm seems like a planet rotating in social space and exerting an irresistible gravitational tug on certain urban psyches. For some, it may tug on a primal urge to get back to the land. They satisfy the urge by helping a few hours, a day, a weekend. For others closely connected with Gayle or me in other lives, our living on and working the farm seems to evoke wonder, even bewilderment. "How could you be doing such a thing?" Still others, especially those who have experienced farm living themselves, understand how much there is to do, and they pitch in whenever they come by with whatever we need at the moment.

The day the old Ford tractor kept stalling, farmer-friend Dave Slagle just happened to be visiting with his family. "Sounds like a fuel problem," he said.

The fuel tank sat above the engine and fed the motor by gravity. We removed the tank, cleaned it out, and solved the problem. It took less than an hour. When I had trouble connecting my new cider-shed wiring, a friend came over, located the problem at the circuit box, and corrected it. What he did in half an hour might have taken me hours to figure out and then fix. And the help is mutual. Another friend couldn't start a pump he'd borrowed to clean out his septic tank. I had used that pump and knew its peculiarities, so I helped him pump out his tank.

While helping neighbors is more important in isolated rural communities than in cities where mechanics and spare parts are near at hand, it is certainly not unique to country living. But the volunteers who come to make cider come for reasons larger than meeting the practical needs of our farm; they come to participate in a community ritual.

Our first regular pressing volunteers were two women of my generation. They had settled in Rio Oscuro after many years of service in a religious order, including ten years of teaching in Bangladesh. Celeste Miller had trained as a Jungian analyst. Sarita Pene had a degree in biology. When I met them, both were employed in a sheltered work program for retarded men and women. Celeste counseled and Sarita ran the greenhouse. Then they left those jobs and took up weaving and started a bed-and-breakfast. One year they trekked in the Himalayas. Another year Celeste enrolled in a dream workshop in Mexico. Celeste was from Iowa; when she found out that I had attended the writers' workshop at the University of Iowa, she asked me to lead an evening writing group in the winter in Rio Oscuro. Lots of people talked about writing, she said, and this would help them all. I demurred; I was having trouble with my own writing, and I did not feel I could help anyone else. But Celeste would not take no for an answer.

"You have an MFA from the best writing program in the country," she said. "Of course you can help us." She said she would recruit the students and do whatever organizing was necessary. Finally I agreed, and as the months passed I realized how much the stories and essays we shared were enriching my life.

At the last session of the workshop in the spring, Sarita said she and Celeste would like to help me make cider. I said that would be fine, and left it at that. Then that fall we had a bumper crop of apples, and it was clear that I would need help, and it would have to come from outside the family for the first time. Sarita called at the beginning of September; when was I going to start pressing, she asked. I said as soon as I found some help. But they were going to help, she said; didn't I remember? I said I couldn't afford to pay very much. No, no, she said; they didn't want to be paid, they just wanted to help.

They arrived at nine o'clock on the first Friday in September, and as I showed them what to do they showed me new ways of working together. I started them at the grinder making pomace. I had written out the recipe for the first pressing, which included the varieties we would use and the number of bushels of each. I showed them where each variety was stacked: Jonathan, Yellow Transparent, Yellow Delicious, and an unknown early red, and I carried some of them over to the grinder. Each box had to be lifted to the pressing stand, and from there the good apples went into the hopper and the culls went into the box on the floor, for the geese.

"Can you manage the boxes, or shall I lift them for you?"

Sarita laughed. "We can manage, Harvey."

As soon as they filled the first barrel with pomace, we were ready to press. As I unfolded the cloth for the first rack and set the square stainless steel form on it, Sarita was already scooping up the first bucket of pomace. Then she or Celeste moved to the other side of the press to steady the rack while I dumped the pomace into the form. Then together we leveled the mound of pomace, I removed the form, and we folded over the cloth to make the first pillow of pomace. As I put on another rack and another cloth, Sarita dug out another bucketful of pomace from the barrel. And so it went with setting up clean bottles in the filling tray, capping, rinsing, labeling, unloading the press. They had never made cider before, but they anticipated every move needed before I asked.

When the grinder wasn't running or the juice pump filling bottles, we talked. We talked about their teaching in Bangladesh, about selling their house in Santa Fe and building a solar house in Rio Oscuro, about little power struggles at the sheltered workshop, about Sarita's life growing up on a farm in Montana, about protecting the small farms in our valley, about people who needed help. And about politics. The more we worked together and the more we talked, the more I enjoyed being with these women who years ago left the religious order they had joined in their youth but had never learned how to stop helping and serving people.

Finally, Sarita asked, quietly, "And how is Marni?"

"Holding her own," I said. "The pain doesn't stop, but the baby seems healthy. She's due next month." And I told them about Marni coming up and Rick playing "Blackbird" to the baby inside Marni on his new guitar.

"Is there anything we can do to help?" said Celeste.

I thanked her, I thanked them both. We're just waiting, I said. And then they began grinding for the last pressing of the day.

Toward the end of the season Sarita wrote about us grayhaired cider makers for a seniors' magazine. A photographer friend took pictures of the process from all the angles he could think of—through the juice cascading down the press, the juice in cups rising to our lips for the ritual tasting and toasting before bottling, the juice filling the bottles, the labeling of the juice bottles. From the dozens of images of our cider making we helped Sarita pick out six for the article. Neither text nor slides, however, impressed the editor; he rejected the submission without comment. Here's one passage in the article that I think of when I want to be reminded why people are drawn here to Obscurana.

When Celeste and I taught in Bangladesh, I learned that the word for juice was *rosh*. One day I heard a Bengali use it, but the context seemed wrong. I told him I thought *rosh* meant juice. He became fiery and passionate. "No! It is more than that. It is the heart of the language, it is the soul of the music, it is the beat of the dance. It is everything. It is everything."

I look into the golden liquid. It is everything. It is everything, to do what you want, to do good things and do them with good people. I see that this is what I want to do, to be with friends, to throw the apples into the chopper one by one, mantras of Jonathan, McIntosh, Winesap.

WHEN GAYLE and I moved here, to this farm sloping northward down to the Rio Oscuro, we saw wooden crosses on each of the peaks around us. The cross on the peak behind us was commissioned by Victoria for Father Meyers. Atop the peak on the other side of the river three brothers put up a cross for their mother. Just up the highway there is a cross on Barrancos Blancos, above the San Ysidro Cemetery.

And down the acequia just beyond Gayle's studio, in a grove of old, twisted junipers, is another cross and a shrine. The grove, according to what elders from Picuris Pueblo told Father Meyers, was sacred to their tribe. To honor the site he put up a cross, built a niche against a wall of rough basalt boulders and faced with chips of pink-and-white lapidolite mined on Pueblo lands, and ordered the statue of the saint that sits in the niche to this day. I call her *Nuestra Señora de las Huertas*, Our Lady of the Orchards. Around the niche were flower beds outlined with the same pink-and-white rocks. In these beds were vases of earthenware, brightly painted, for more flowers. And inside the niche, above the head of the Virgin, were lights, two bulbs in brass sockets connected to wires running to the house.

Looking at the shrine today it is hard to sense the pastor's vision. The cross is lying on the ground. Branches of the junipers have grown over the niche and over the flower beds, to the very edge of the acequia. Heavy snows have bent some branches almost to the ground. The vases are broken, the flower beds dried out. One sickly rose struggles on, and in the sagebrush are some stunted iris. I took down the rotting wires when we first came, and now we can only imagine how the shrine looked with the lights on.

Surely Father Meyers illuminated the shrine on Christmas Eve, joining its beacon to the luminarias and the farolitos all over the valley. Perhaps he turned on the lights while the orchards were blooming, to encourage pollination, or during the summers, to encourage the fruit to ripen. Perhaps on feast days Corina and Annelise and Victoria put fresh flowers in the vases. Perhaps the peones cleaning the acequia every spring stopped here for a moment to bless themselves. And perhaps the mayordomo of la Acequia Ultima, after the spring cleaning, after he had turned the river water into the channel and followed the flow along the road, forking out the old leaves and branches, then sent his helper to follow the water around the edge of the hill while he came up here to wait, to wait with *Nuestra Señora de las Huertas y los Indios* to bless the new water in the old ditch.

To me, sacred ground is the orchard that *Nuestra Señora* holds summer and winter in her white stone gaze, this congregation of fruit trees and *la tierra*, the earth on which they stand.

I believe each people and perhaps each person should choose what to hold sacred.

IN OUR own time Robert "Ra" Paulette, a stonemason and veteran of Vietnam, trekked miles of rocky desert slopes and plains around our village in search of a site to build his own shrine. Above the Rio Grande, just below the top of Black Mesa, he found it, a sandstone face with a view of the river, the valley, the many peaks topped with crosses, and in the distance the Sangre de Cristo, Blood of Christ, New Mexico's highest mountains. For three years Ra hiked up to his site almost every day to cut, to carve, to sand, to polish, to plaster, and to heal himself. He called his shrine the Cave of the Chambers of the Heart. When he finished he invited his friends to share this space.

Over the next three years friends told friends about Ra's cave until hundreds and hundreds of people, some from far away, were visiting each year. They filled up one guest book and then another with words of thanks and praise. And, as in other shrines, people left tokens of prayer and blessing. Climbing the trail to the cave became a pilgrimage, to perform alone or share with family and friends.

But pilgrims are also people, people who cross private lands without permission, who block private roads and driveways with their cars, who trample flowers, break fences. The neighbors complained to the Bureau of Land Management that Congress has entrusted with the care of these public slopes and plains. The cave was becoming a public nuisance, they said, and the managers had better start doing some managing. The local office of the BLM called a public meeting to which Ra and the offended neighbors were invited. By this time Ra had his own problems keeping the cave intact under so much traffic, however loving it was. He proposed to backfill the cave and restore the site. The BLM agreed to pay him for his work. The immediate neighbors seemed to welcome the return of their privacy. But over the months that followed the decision, many who knew Ra's cave felt they were losing something of value that would never be replaced.

IT IS the Sunday before Ra plans to close and begin to backfill his shrine. I hike up one last time, to show the cave to artist friend and neighbor Jim Gilbert. Jim brings his camcorder. We are not the only visitors, and we wait outside, with the birds attending the wooden feeder set on a pole. Red faces with red breasts, striped faces with striped breasts, all feeding, hopping around the feeder, flitting from feeder to nearby junipers, to the ground, back and forth. Again onto the feeder. Tiny birds, four to five inches long, varying from an almost iridescent fire-engine red, the red of a tropical bird, to deeper, duller scarlet reds— signs of maturity or genetic variation? The birds do not say. They do their flitting from juniper to ground to feeder to water pan, oblivious to their benefactor's plans.

Ra has painted a sign on a board by the entrance: "Share. Share the Heart Cave. I will come up to feed and water birds." Under it is a galvanized barrel of birdseed. The sign will probably come down when Ra has finished backfilling and sealing the cave. I wonder how long it will take the birds to realize that this habitat has been altered, returned to the dry, eroding desert it used to be?

Now we go inside. Jim turns on his camcorder, starts in the back-most chamber, moves slowly up the first white carved and braided column, across the braided ceiling, down the back wall.

I open the guest book and read aloud.

"Thank you for creating this beautiful place. May God bless you and your talents."

"I can't say how much it touches me."

"This is a creation beyond my imagination."

"The beauty and peace I find here I will carry with me always."

"You have created a song."

"A sacred place of the heart . . ."

"The peace of our mother . . ."

"When you travel on to whatever is next for you, you leave behind a sacred gift for our children."

I stop reading and tear a blank sheet from the guest book and start to list the items in the niches, on the ledges and shelves, and hanging on the walls, what people from the villages around here have carried to Ra's cave, as gifts and offerings.

The Inventory of Offerings
    Vancouver BC T-shirt
    3 wristwatches
    two wooden crucifixes
    picture of Mary and the baby Jesus
    coins, many of them quarters
    a plastic butterfly
    rocks

2 bundles of weeds

feather

Indian corn

bark with moss and feather

miniature Bible

Bible verses

Alcoholics Anonymous creed

Jesus & Mary medallion

wind pipes

Little Brother medal

Indian fetish sticks

a grouping of seashells

a key

carved Madonna

a single seashell

Chinese statue

picture of Jesus with a candle in front of it

gourd

more candles

rusted bolts

potsherds

flakes from stone tools

Indian pouches

braided belt

deer horns

turquoise chain with black crucifix

gold crucifix

silver earrings with stars

cholla cactus branch with weeds in its holes

Budweiser beer label

dollar bill

rusted tobacco can

color snapshot of a young boy, about 5

picture of Walt Disney

prayer card—"Lord give me the strength . . ."

rosette design on stone

crystal
feather with beads
driftwood
curl of bark with piñon comb and needles
shotgun shell casing

When Ra refills each chamber with the soft rock and dirt he had dug out to create the cave, I wonder if he will bury all these things in place.

AUGUST 1, 1992. For more than a year, Marni had been giving all of herself to her fight with cancer, but today she wanted to take time out to celebrate Peter's thirty-first birthday. And she wanted to do something special that he would like: an overnight campout in the mountains together with nine-month-old Trevor. They would drive up to the farm from Albuquerque, and her brother Mark and his wife, Jacque, and their four-year-old, Corin, would drive down from Denver, and we would have a joint birthday party for Peter and me. I had always liked birthday parties, and I was pleased to have a son-in-law with the same birthday to share one with me. Afterwards the two young families would drive up to a campsite.

As soon as we had embraced and Marni was inside and before I could say anything, Marni handed me a letter. "I finished it two weeks ago, but it's pretty much up-to-date," she said. "It answers all the questions people have been asking about me. I mailed out a lot of copies. This is yours."

I opened it and started to read. "Maybe you want to save it for later, Dad." I studied my daughter's face for some clue about what she had written, but all I could see was her frailness, how thin her face was. I thanked her—I did not know what else to do.

Gayle had made two cakes. On mine she put candles for decades. On the cake for Peter, half my age, there were more. Now, remembering, I wish there had been a third cake, one for Marni, for a birthday too many months away.

But what Marni wanted was some miso broth, and I offered to

make it. She told me to boil the water, then put in a tablespoon of miso and let it cook for just fifteen seconds. I measured, I timed, I stirred. Then I poured the broth into a bowl. She tasted it. Too bland. How much miso had I put in? Let me do it again, I said. No, she said, that would be all right. And was that all she was going to eat? She wasn't hungry, she said. "I wish you would let me fix it again for you."

"No, that's all right, Dad."

Soup. All I could do for her, and even that I couldn't do well.

We sang "Happy Birthday," we opened gifts. I gave Peter a birthday bouquet of everlasting from Rose Mary and Stan, my neighbors at the farmers' market. Marni took one bite of birthday cake. Then Mark said it might be a good idea to start up the mountain so they would have plenty of time to find a good campsite. Marni looked so tired I asked if she wouldn't rather spend the night here rather than try to sleep on the ground. No, she said; she wanted to camp; her birthday present for Peter. So we said good-bye. Tomorrow, after the campout, Mark and Jacque and Corin would go on toward Denver; Marni and Peter and Trevor would see us again on their way home.

Now Gayle and I read Marni's letter.

July 1992

Dear Family and Friends,

I have so much to say and so many people with whom I want to share my life, please excuse this format.

How are each and every one of you? I think about you often, obviously more often than you hear from me. I hope that your health is good, your spirits are high and your love flows freely.

We are doing great! Spring brought a wonderful change for us. Seeing the rebirth of the planet with all the hues of healthy/healing green brought Love and Joy to our lives—after a very difficult, dreary and depressing winter. God/Nature is so wonderful that there can be no doubt as to whether miracles exist. Our personal little miracle, Trevor, is full of life and joy, and I wish that everyone could meet him.

Peter and I are still very much in love. We have been through a lot

*in our first year together, and I thank God each day for our relation-
ship. Yes, fairy tales do come true. Peter is everything I had hoped for
in a companion and much more. Isn't it amazing how just the universe is? I don't think I could have gotten through this cancer ordeal
without Peter's constant love and support. And certainly, we wouldn't
have had a baby if I'd been diagnosed any sooner. Not to mention
that it would have ruined our beautiful wedding. All in all, I am one
of the luckiest people in the world. We are very happy. (So don't you
dare say to yourself "Poor dear Marni, she is so unfortunate.")*

*We live in a modest two-bedroom house in a decent neighbor-
hood in the middle of town. The living room is filled with wonderful colors and art and toys all over the floor. Every room has plants
in it, and there is always a bowl of fruit on the table. (My mother
said that was a sign of true wealth.) My sister, Susan, just made us
new kitchen curtains, and I baked a batch of cookies to celebrate.
Susan is also an important support person in my life. She runs er-
rands for me and comes over just to share her glowing love.*

*Our backyard is large with a small patio and several nice trees.
Peter planted a wonderful garden and put up some netting for
shade. The squash and tomatoes are starting to ripen, and my flowers are blooming.*

*Trevor will be nine months July 9th; he is a BIG boy. He will be
tall like a Frauenglass. Trevy (for short) crawls at a good pace,
scoots all over in his walker, stands up holding on to anything,
walks around furniture and eats most everything. The day before
Peter's first Father's Day Trevor cut his first tooth (on top); the second one is coming soon. It is so difficult to push those teeth out, but
he's got an excellent drool system to ease the process.*

*The most wonderful thing for me is to witness Trevor's growing
attachment to Peter and me. He is learning to reciprocate affec-
tion—with arms stretched wide, wet baby kisses and a few pats on
Mommy's head. He likes to pat and rub my new hair (about 3/4"
long). Trevor also discovered peek-a-boo without any prompting,
and he loves to clap his hands to music. Aaahhh, what a little gem!!!*

*Baby's are truly a full-time job. Fortunately, I have some help
each day. This allows me to go to appointments, do my physical*

therapy and meditate or rest. Healing is also a full-time job. It's like the old union song, you've got to do it by yourself. The universe has sent me some wonderful people who donate their time and therapeutic work out of the goodness of their hearts. I receive Reiki healing twice a week from two different friends; this is a type of hands-on energy flow from God. I receive physical therapy (also using energy flow) on Sundays, and my chiropractor sees me as often as needed. I also had two machines donated to me by a girlfriend: one for color therapy and relaxation and the other for Rife Electrical Frequency therapy, which was shown in the 30s and again in the 70s to kill cancer cells.

I am also on a regimen of physical therapy twice daily to stimulate neurological functioning, strengthen my skinny little war-torn body, and thereby remove the pain in my lower back and hips. We have changed our diet to low-fat—very little chicken and fish, and no dairy (except for an occasional frozen yogurt). Basically, we avoid sugar and caffeine and eat lots of fresh fruit, steamed vegetables and whole grains. This is a diet for all to consider. I am also taking Chinese herbs to strengthen my body and reduce the size of my liver. Next month a Chinese herbal doctor will start me on strong anti-cancer herbs. All my therapies, new friends and doctors have come together, once again in a miraculous fashion.

My prognosis? Well, if I believed my medical doctors, then I should die in a week or two—HAAAH! Fat chance! I'm going to throw a "Beat the Prognosis" party and laugh in death's face; I'll die when I'm good and ready. The extremely large tumor in my breast (6 inches long & 3 inches wide) is GONE. The tumor in my arm pit lymph nodes (size of a golf ball) is GONE. The lesions in my spine and pelvis probably aren't tumors since there has been no growth in 3 months. The lesions in my brain, well, I guess I drank too much beer in college. And my liver (that makes me look 4 months pregnant) is large because of a blood flow problem and chemotherapy toxicity, not because of tumor growth. So there!

Can you understand what I'm saying, where I'm coming from, and where I'm going? I have been very sick, mostly due to the

chemotherapy, but now I am recovering. I am not going to die soon.
I am healing physically, mentally, emotionally and spiritually.
God's love (i.e., the Universal Energy) is my guide. My life, our
lives, are full of love and joy. Please do not send me sympathy and
sorrow; I don't want it. Send me love, healing energy, laughter and
more love. Send me funny pictures and jokes, share stories about
healings with me, come visit and we'll play with Trevor.
Remember, Life is good and Life is love.

All my Love,
with a big, warm hug,

Marni

P.S. Peter and Trevor say "Hi!"

AFTER THE birthday party, Gayle and I talked about the trip we
had planned for the coming week. We were flying east, to visit
family and friends and help celebrate Aunt Anne's fifty-fifth
wedding anniversary. Aunt Anne, my mother's sister, was also my
godmother, my only living mother. We had missed her big fiftieth
anniversary. She was not well. Who knew how many more an-
niversaries she would have? We had promised, we had the tickets.

Anne called once a month to find out how Marni was doing. If
she could see how Marni had looked at the party, I thought, she
would probably not want us to leave. But if we didn't go, Marni
would be very unhappy; I was sure of that. We went back and
forth: stay and wait, or go and trust? Both ways were right. We
did not decide.

The next morning. Marni and Peter and little Trevor returned
from the mountains. Marni had not slept all night. The air mattress, the cold, the pain; she could not get comfortable. After a
few minutes, she told Peter she wanted to go home. I tried to
bring up the subject of our not going. She wouldn't hear of it.
She got into the car. Trevor was in his car seat. Peter was waiting
to start.

"Give my love to Cousin Sheryl and Amy," she said. "Tell

them—" and she started to cry, "tell them I'm thinking about them." I kissed her. I tried not to cry. "I'll see you when you get back," she said, and they left.

We were gone a week. As soon as we could get out of the Albuquerque airport we drove directly to Marni and Peter's. Marni was lying on the sofa in the living room.

"Hi, Dad," she said. I sat beside her, held her hand. I told her about the trip. There was so much else I wanted to say and no words for it. Eventually she dozed off.

Karen came in from the kitchen. I asked her how Marni was doing.

"The same," she said. "Sleeping a lot."

Andrew was there. He said the University of New Mexico where he ran a laser laboratory had given him compassionate leave so he could help care for his sister. He and Susan had arranged between them that one or the other would be with her all the time now. Earlier in the year, after Peter had used up all of his personal leave in caring for Marni, the small company he worked for sent around an employee memo asking if anyone wanted to give Peter part of their personal leave time so he could continue to be with Marni and still draw his salary. Twenty fellow workers donated leave time.

Reluctantly we drove back to the farm.

And here is where my memories of the days began to get mixed up. I picked fruit and went to the farmers' market. That had to be Saturday. I don't know what day it was when we headed to Albuquerque again. We stopped by to see Bob and Carolyn, to tell them how Marni was. Carolyn asked if we would buy a flowering plant for them to give to Marni. They were being advertised by a nursery in Albuquerque. Could we do that, would it be too much trouble? We said we would be glad to do it, and thanked her.

Albuquerque. We stayed the night with David and Mona Johnson. The next day, was that Sunday? We walked into Marni and Peter's house. The bedroom door was closed. It was the worst night, Karen said. Andrew and Peter were in the bedroom with her. Julie was in with Trevor, putting him down with his bottle.

We sat down. What to do? We got up, went out to the backyard. It was August, it was hot. We walked around the yard. We went back inside. Karen came out of the bedroom. "I would suggest that you go in to her now," she said.

The bedroom. Soft summer light seeps through the curtain. The potted yellow flowers on the dresser. And the pink and white and yellow and purple blossoms of everlasting. From the tape player the sounds of water falling, birds crying, wind, rain in the rain forest. Marni, my daughter, in the rain forest. Hollow-cheeked, arctic-white skin. And so thin, all but weightless, her head hardly dents the pillows. Thirty-one. Only thirty-one.

Around the bed. Peter, kneeling, holding her. Andrew on the other side, holding her hand. Husband, brother. Next to Andrew, me. Next to me, Gayle. Next to Peter, Marni's friend Julie. Next to Julie, Karen.

Her breathing. Gritty, as if scraped over a bed of rocks. Each breath is pulled out of a cave. Struggling up the wall, grasping for places to hold, to keep from falling back. One breath, then another, yet another. Never have I heard breathing like that.

Now Peter climbs up on the bed, holds her head against his chest. Andrew holds her on the other side. I hold a leg. Gayle holds a foot. Julie holds a foot. Karen, the other leg. The six of us breathe our simple breaths. The sounds of water, birds, rain-stick music. And Marni breathes her hard breathing of this morning, breathing on Morningside but bound into the night. Bob and Carolyn's chrysanthemums on the dresser, the bouquet of everlasting wrapped by Rose Mary beside them.

"It's all right, darling, you can let go now," Peter says. "It's all right, it's all right." And her breathing changes, becomes soft, gentle like calm water lapping the hull of a small boat, slow, restful, passing, intervals longer and longer between each breath, and then, at last, quiet.

Marni.

People arrive. Susan with Dita. Barbara Pepper, minister, midwife, healer, consoler. Juliana, Marni's friend. Jana, Susan's friend. We gather around the bed. Barbara lights the sage for smudging. Says prayers. The battles are over. We must become instruments of peace. We hold each other. We leave the room. Juliana dresses the wasted body of beautiful Marni, her once fellow ballet dancer, for the final time. Susan weeps, says, "I want to go with her," then she and Jana go in, and the three sit with this sister and friend.

Time passes. We talk. We eat pizza. We hold Trevor. Trevor, Trevor. And Peter, Peter. The men arrive with a stretcher to take the body of Marni to be cremated. They go into the bedroom and carry her out. Jana follows them, carrying the bouquet of everlasting. She places it on the stretcher and says, "Good-bye, body of Marni."

TREVOR SAYS he is three and a half, but for all I know he could be two hundred or thousands. He could be as old as the river before us gurgling its winter song. He's always asking questions, always listening. "What is this car for?" he wonders, lying on his stomach on the floor of the wooden tram car, swinging it back and forth on its cable. I explain how people pull the car out over the middle of the river and put a meter into the water to measure the flow. "Can we ride on it?" I tell him the car is chained to the steel tower, and point to the chain and the padlock. "Why is it chained?" I tell him that the people who measure the river think it could be dangerous to ride the car. They don't want anyone to get hurt or to damage the car. He swings back and forth. "When can we ride on it?" Maybe someday. He does not ask me what he will ask his father over breakfast when they get home: "When is my mommy coming home? When can she stop being dead and come home?" He has large brown eyes and long lashes. His soft brown hair that his daddy cuts, as he told us, hangs over his ears and his forehead. Now, by the river with me, he smiles. "I want to stay here forever with you, Grandpa." And he swings and swings.

This morning we had done our chores together. Scratch grain to the chickens. With a mittened hand smaller than a duck egg Trevor scooped a tablespoonful of grain from the bucket and offered it to the black hen with iridescent green and purple markings. She eyed the hand and its offering, stepping to the right, then the left, one foot to the other. The orange beak bobbed up, down, under, around, and peck, peck, peck, corn, sorghum, wheat, one grain at a time. Then we let the screaming geese into the garden to continue their winter weeding. We gave oats and alfalfa to the horse.

Trevor took off his mittens as I held him up to the great brown flank. "He's warm." Yes, I said, alive, like us. Then I broke the ice in the water barrel, and we went into the cider shed to get apples for Trevor and me. This was our winter routine.

Now he swings and swings, and if he dreams of his mother, he does not tell me. He was only ten months old when she died, but old enough, of course, for his mind to be alive to her presence. And her absence. He knows the story of her cancer, her fight for life, and her choice to give him life. His father, Peter, has told him, and Trevor also knows the word *death*. He knows that Xeno, the other horse, whom he had rubbed and sat astride, died last year and is buried in our orchard. He remembers Xeno. He does not remember his mother.

Trevor for me is both himself and Marni. He holds my hand as we walk out of our small bosque and follow the road toward the house.

November three years ago Gayle and I scattered Marni's ashes on the farm, the half cup Peter sent up with Andrew in a baby-food jar: "Earth's Best Baby Food," certified organically grown sweet potatoes. I had kept the ashes in Gayle's desk in the living room and looked at them every day for three months, till Marni's birthday. Gayle and I stood on the porch. I didn't know where to start.

"Marni loved my flowers," Gayle said. "When they come up again next year we can think of her."

So we gave a bit of ash to the flowers for the next year. Then some in the acequia for the fields beyond. Then over grapes

Marni had helped us prune, then around selected trees in the orchard she had picked, and the last by the pole barn, where we feed the horse, where we lift our eyes to the hills, where Gayle sings "Amazing Grace."

Perhaps this year some of Marni's atoms have found their way into our apple trees as the apples found their way into her, our cider being the last nourishment she took. I cannot really account for the atoms, whether they're in apples or blossoms or branches. But she is here.

That evening Trevor says he wants a bath, so I fill the tub and give him the floating toys we keep for grandchildren. He lies in the warm water, smiling, sits up, holds the plastic car under the water, runs it around the tub, lies back again. He smiles. "Grandpa," he says, "I want to stay here forever."

I already know how I will feel on Monday when Trevor goes home. I will walk down to the animals alone. My hand will be empty.

OUR GRANDCHILDREN were not born when we came here thirteen years ago. Jessica, two months older than Trevor, now calls from her home on the east side of the state to find out what the dogs and cats and the horse and Gayle and I are doing on her farm. When she visits she wants to feed her animals, no matter what time of day, and can barely stand to wait till morning. She screams as the geese approach her, grabs my leg for security, but refuses to leave until we're done or her daddy, Jamie, shows up.

Corin, Mark and Jacque's son who is now six and has just changed his name to Peter, pressed his first cider with us last fall. He ground apples, stacked racks, pumped up the press, filled bottles. Only eighteen gallons? On the next pressing, as we tilted the stand loaded with racks this way and that way to get out the last drops, Peter was shouting and jumping up and down. "More, more!" After we finished, washed and swept and put everything away, it was time for lunch. We started up to the house, carrying a jug of the fresh cider, but Peter stopped me to say, "You are the best grandpa in the world!"

Some days after the snow has lain so long on the north slopes that it seems permanent, and we have burnt all but a few armfuls of the wood we gathered and cut and stacked last summer, I think of the grandchildren. On those days I would like them here, to go down to the orchard with me and chop the ice on the horse's bucket, to chop more wood, to carry the water to the chickens and carry the wood in to the stove. It is not what they can carry, or the kindling they can gather that I think of. And it is not any dream of them growing up and becoming farmers, farmers on this land, that brings them to mind. It is wanting to share the farm with them.

And sometimes, living with these apple trees, I feel I am becoming one of them. According to the Gaia hypothesis that is not so strange—earth, animals, grasses, microbes, clouds, cells, molecules, and atoms, and all the spirits animating them, are one. Perhaps this is why so many people come to visit and work with us on this farm. They want to smell the growing, they want to feel the branches and blossoms, prune trees, climb ladders and pick fruit, plant and weed and irrigate. They want to feel a part of the one. And then sit at Gayle's bountiful table and break bread, and tell us how this life seems to them. They come because they need an exercise in humbleness, says Robert Francis Johnson, a friend from Santa Fe; humble, humus, of the earth, earthy . . .

THE GRAND inventory of all the fruit trees in the orchard that I had talked about, planned, started again and again, and finally accepted as an expectation that would never be fulfilled in this lifetime is taken up by a man who appears out of nowhere, calls himself "Chaos," loves charts, and watches stars with his ten-year-old "adopted" grandson, Nick. Together they locate every tree on a grid and ask me to walk with them and identify each by variety. Chaos then enters the data on his laptop computer and produces a printout of the orchard. Using this printout we learn for the first time how many trees of each variety we have, and how many unknown varieties we must make up our own names for. Now it is possible to estimate in advance our expected crop, to direct the pickers to specific trees for specific fruit needed for cider each week, and to record how many bushels are picked from each tree and the picking date or dates. With this inventory and the harvest records, a cidermaster could both see the orchard as a whole and know it perfectly over time, variety by variety.

THE TWO ganders have taken over where the kidnapped and presumably killed mother goose left off. The white walks first, and the gray Toulouse walks last. The goslings march between, in and out of the acequia, always staying together. Now the goslings are under the pear trees, nipping blades of grass and leaves and stems of small weeds. I bring them water, and the guardians try to stop me from getting too close. I watch them graze and run around each other. So much goes on here that I want to be present to witness. Then I remember: I have picking to do for the Los Alamos market tomorrow.

THE WATER sings its way down the lateral east of the road. It sings the brook song, softly, steady, relentless, like a spring coming out of the high mountains, a reenactment here on the farm. I like it, and listen—which still does not pick our apricots, or the first of the July apples in the orchard below. All right, I say, stop watching, stop listening, move back to the ladder. This is hard! I pass a monarch butterfly fondling a purple flower. The Dane lies in the lane, cradling his head in his paw. He watches me. I watch the chickens in the next field. The black crowned Polish bantam tries to mount a red Rhode Island half a size larger. I start picking again.

Epilogue

Tengo Deudas

And forgive us our debts, as
we forgive our debtors.
. . . .
For if ye forgive men their
trespasses, your heavenly Father
will also forgive you:
But if ye forgive not men their
trespasses, neither will your Father
forgive your trespasses. (Matt. 6:12, 14-15)

MANY WINTERS HAVE passed since Uncle Bill asked why we had "chosen such a hard path." He did not respond to last year's Christmas card. He is not writing anymore, according to Richard, his son. Uncle Bill worked his way around the world on tramp steamers at seventeen. He taught high school for twenty-five years. When he was fired at fifty for his politics in his twenties, he went back to school and became a child psychologist. And he pursued his love for Chinese food. Every time we visited, we ended up in the kitchen of some restaurant in Chinatown. Finally, when his wife came down with an incurable ailment, he gave up everything to care for her. Now Uncle Bill himself is in a nursing home. He has his lucid moments, Richard wrote, but he can no longer correspond.

I had written in the card that we were still farming. Richard must have misread my handwriting. At the end of his letter he wrote, "And what is 'forming?' You say you are still 'forming'; what does that mean?" Richard, my cousin, is a retired engineer. He worked for a large aerospace company. We have never corresponded. But I want to start, and this is as good a place as any.

Cousin, your question is well taken. I wrote "farming," but it could be "forming" as well because, really, what goes on here is forming and reforming us. These definitions explain the process as well as any I can think of.

The farm is people

is the orchards

is the individual trees

is the sons and daughters and grandsons and granddaughters

is the brothers and sisters

is the aunts and uncles

is the cousins and their husbands and wives

is the friends

is the animals

is the garden and the raspberry patch

is the farmhouse

is the old galvanized corrugated roof of the farmhouse that leaks into one, two, three, four, five, six, seven pots when the rainfall lasts long enough.

The farm is me on the roof with the cordless twelve-volt driver-drill screwing the galvanized corrugated panels to the joists and cross members where the old roofing nails have popped out and will not be popped into rotted holes again; me on the roof seeking good wood under the old metal to screw into, to keep the unruly, independent panels, the shamelessly unreliable panels from lifting their edges again in the next rain, under the next snow, or any other rain or snow in the next year, the next five or ten years, or anytime on my watch, for as long as I charge myself with fixing this roof, keeping the leaks out of the kitchen, the drips off Gayle's word processor, or until we are ready to replace the corrugated galvanized roofing with permanent, guaranteed, and expensive ceramic-coated panels.

The farm is us, we are the farm. The farm is those who came before us, who lived here, who put a galvanized roof over the sod roof to stop its leaking, who saved the bits of string and wrapping paper, the empty candy boxes and candy wrappers, the egg cartons, the catalogs from Aldens, the *Look*s and *Saturday Evening Post*s and *Colliers,* and *Life*s, from the first issue in 1937.

It is the priest who read German, Spanish, English, and Latin (especially Latin—the *Gallia est omnis divisa in partes tres* . . . and *vini, vidi, vicum,* which conquerors have been writing back to Rome and Madrid and London and Washington forever, whether true or not) in which he said prayers to Jesus, Maria, y José and Señor Yahweh or the ineffable. ·

The farm is all the neighbor children who picked cherries here all day for ten cents and a picture of Father Meyers with his Great Danes. It is the planters of fruit trees, the plowers and harvesters, and the cider makers before us. It is Friedrich and Victoria and Corina picking grapes and making wine and the wine they made, and the graves of a hundred-hundred whiskey bottles we uncovered above the house. And this is only the beginning.

The farm is our guest Rick, the Albuquerque hotel manager who broke the handle of the maul splitting wood and then so maddened Gayle's cutting horse with his English riding technique that the horse next day threw Gayle into the barbed-wire fence.

The farm is Gayle: running down the ditch bank in her long nightgown in heavy rain, the acequia full to overflowing, slipping in the wet grass and mud, to open the gate to the orchard and drain off the excess water; digging and chopping roots alongside ten peones so we could line the eight hundred feet of this acequia with a coated fabric that would finally stop the leaks, at least for a few years; planting in the garden and along the ditch by the house, tending the sprouts and new plants, carrying hoses and directing water to daisies, cosmos, snapdragons, and rosebushes; and standing all day in the kitchen peeling, pitting, drying, or packing into fruit jars our peaches, apricots, pears, and tomatoes.

The farm is Marni finding Peter and Peter finding Marni at the studio tour. It is Peter and Marni heavy in her seventh month with Trevor, and our Rick playing his guitar for us and the baby. It is the hummingbird who visited Gayle in the greenhouse after Marni died. It is Gayle and I spreading Marni's ashes under the great Jonathan and then Gayle by the pole barn facing the hills singing a hymn.

The farm, finally, is sharing when we are able even when we are not certain what we are sharing. Cecilia Chang, a computer consultant of Chinese descent, bought a painting from Gayle at the New Mexico Arts and Craft Fair in Albuquerque. Later she called Gayle. She was hosting some teachers from China. Could she bring them up to the farm on Sunday, perhaps to help with the harvest? Of course.

Cecilia brought two families with children, and we went right down to the orchard. While I was demonstrating how to use the picking bags and ladders, with Gloria translating, Nam Soon and Sung Soo Park appeared. Nam had been my most enthusiastic student in two evening courses I taught at the community college. Sung Soo, her husband, was an instructor in physics and electronic technology. One day Nam had climbed on the roof of the cider shed and picked twelve baskets of mulberries in the time it took me or anyone else to pick four. On this day they had brought us a plate of vegetarian sushi. And they had a camcorder; they wanted to send sounds and pictures of us and our farm to their families in South Korea.

We introduced Nam and her husband, Sung Soo, to Cecilia, the teachers, and their families. Then Cecilia and her visitors started picking, and Nam took me aside. I had never seen this cheerful young woman so unhappy.

"What's the matter?"

She put her hand to her mouth and whispered, "Do you know they are communists?"

I liked Nam very much. I wanted her to always be happy when she came here. But about wrongs that had been done and were still being done in her native country I could do nothing.

"Nam, I do not know the politics of these teachers and their families," I said. "I know they come from a communist country. But here they are visitors, and they are helping us pick apples. That's all." And I smiled at her.

"Okay," she said, and she tried to smile back. She and Sung Soo went off with the camcorder. I do not know if she recorded any scenes of Chinese teachers or their children in our apple trees, but when we all sat down for lunch, Nam and Sung Soo sat at the other end of the picnic table from the pickers from China.

The farm is also Thanksgiving, many Thanksgivings and other gatherings with everybody here at two long tables, children, brothers and sisters, parents, aunts and uncles, Gayle's Uncle Bob who is gone, her mother, Ione, gone, and Marni, her ashes, her spirit, in the trees.

Tengo Amor

What you give, write in the sand.
What you receive, carve it in rock.
—Polish folk saying

According to Mitchell Feigenbaum, one developer of chaos theory, a predictable or probable outcome may turn unpredictable or improbable because of a small, even minute deviation from the norm that appears early in the development process. Call it a trigger. A telephone call. A kind word from a stranger. A fall from a ladder. A prize, a loss, a fear, a fright, a delight.

An insignificant aberration magnified by time can produce unintended, unexpected turbulence in the flow. Earthquakes come from tiny stresses, pressures compounded over millennia. Clouds, storms, hurricanes—all start small.

Tengo Deudas II

I am one who started small, but by now I have accumulated great debts. I have broken all the commandments, and not just once. Taken what was not mine, coveted, lied and laid lies upon lies, made promises I did not keep, dishonored what I loved and whom I loved and who loved me.

I have said I was sorry a hundred-hundred times, and cried and grieved at the harm I have done. But my sorries have been too often just words, as sounding brass or a tinkling cymbal. Being sorry, as Gayle has reminded me more than once, means you never will do that again. If it costs you your life, you still try to keep your promise. (Or, at the very least, you talk about it.)

Tengo Amor

But I have love for small farms and for the families who live on them and work them. I have a warm place in my heart for all the people who encourage small farmers by buying from them at farmers' markets. I appreciate more than I can say those who come to help pick, to prune, to make cider, and just to give whatever hand is needed. And I am grateful to those who care about protecting the water and the rural land use and who go to meetings and write letters and make phone calls. Small farmers need all the help and encouragement they can get.

I have love for the fruit trees entrusted to our care on this farm. I am grateful to Friedrich and Victoria and Corina and whoever else for planting these fruit trees, for digging the ditches and building the gateways to irrigate the trees. And for those who picked the fruit and pruned the branches and raked and hoed and shoveled those sixty years and more before us, especially the shovelers.

I have love for old farmers who plant trees whose fruit they may never taste in this lifetime. And for people who keep hundred-year-old apple trees. And for people new to the land who start out with old varieties, who set their trees in the traditional way, with room for wildflowers.

I have love for the wildflowers in the orchard that feed and hide the hover flies and wasps till they are ready to feed on the coddling moths and others that would eat our fruit. I have love for the day lilies, the phlox, the iris, the roses, especially the roses, that those before us planted and tended and encouraged to spread along the driveways, along the ditches, under the fruit trees, wherever there was place and water. I have special love for the flowers Gayle has planted and continues to plant along the walk, along the acequia, below the bank, everywhere around the house she can find a few feet of ground, even in the shade under the portal. And I have love beyond measure for Gayle.

Whatever I feel about farming and this farm notwithstanding, without Gayle there would be no flowers, no farm, no farm book. In its best years my farming has brought in only half our income. In its worst, when late frost takes most of our fruit, farming brings in very little. However much I do, it is Gayle's art that has sustained the farm. She has also done her share of shoveling and hoeing, weeding and pruning, and picking and drying and canning vegetables, fruit, jams, and juices. And there is still more she does merely by her being, through her touch.

Tengo Dudas

I doubt that growing fruit and flowers, planting and shoveling or any other of the things we do will save the world. Perhaps Gayle painting and drawing helps, but I can only speak for myself.

I doubt a son of Victoria and Father Meyers will ever appear.

I doubt that my dreamer's eye will ever see this farm as clearly as Gayle's painter's eye.

I doubt that going back to the land will automatically bring people a better life. It's easy to forsake technology and convenience; it's much harder to forsake the desires that spawn them.

I doubt that the cidermaster will ever appear in my lifetime.

I have doubts that I have never spoken of. That the reasons we give for what we do have nothing to do with reality. That we are not even coming close to what is behind what we think are our aspirations, our motives. We go on, blindly, in great ignorance.

ᴏ— —ᴏ

I ONCE doubted that I would find Father Meyers's buried treasure at Obscurana. But that was before I learned where I had to look for it.

Resources

Crawford, Stanley. *A Garlic Testament.* New York: Harper Collins, 1992.

———. *Mayordomo.* Albuquerque: University of New Mexico Press, 1988.

Dillard, Annie. "Teaching a Stone to Talk." In *Teaching a Stone to Talk.* New York: Harper, 1983.

Frost, Robert. "After Apple Picking." In *The Poetry of Robert Frost.* New York: Holt, Rinehart, Winston, 1969.

Fukuoka, Masanobu. *The One-Straw Revolution.* New York: Bantam, 1985.

Govinda, Lama Anagarika. *The Way of the White Cloud.* Boulder, Colo.: Shambhala, 1970.

Granat, Robert. "My Apples." In *Tierra.* El Paso: Cinco Punto, 1989.

Hanh, Thich Nhat. *Being Peace.* Berkeley, Calif.: Parallax, 1987.

Mollison, Bill. *Permaculture Two.* Tyalgum, Australia: Tagari, 1987.

Mollison, Bill, and David Holmgren. *Permaculture One.*
Tyalgum, Australia: Tagari, 1987.

Orton, Vrest. *The American Cider Book.* New York: Noonday,
1973.

Proulx, Annie. *Making the Best Apple Cider.* Pownal, Vt.:
Garden Way, 1980.

Suzuki, Shunryo. *Zen Mind, Beginner's Mind.* New York:
Weatherhill, 1975.

Williams, Terry Tempest. *Refuge.* New York: Vintage, 1991.

Coda

In the Attic, in the Darkness

When the mason was ready to begin
the interior chimney, he carried a high
pile of bricks into the kitchen, and sacks
of cement, sand, and a tub to mix
the mortar in. He drew two buckets of water
from the outside well, then paused
to measure the task.

The house rose two tall stories
with a full attic tucked under
a steeply slanted roof. The carpenter,
a friend from a farm a half mile north
along a muddy rutted road, was even now
cutting a hole in the shingled roof

which the mason, if all went well,
intended late that afternoon to raise
a chimney through.

The carpenter waved. "I'll be through
in a couple more minutes," he called down;
"then it's all yours." The mason smiled,
picked up the buckets of water,
and carried them inside. He laid out
his tools, then stepped into
the corner and looked straight up
to sight the chimney's path.

He should have seen a tunnel of sky,
but past the hole in the kitchen
ceiling and the hole in the ceiling
of the second story bedroom it was dark.
He knew the carpenter was done because
he heard him making a cautious way
down the tall ladder from the eaves.

The light through the kitchen windows
was winter gray and the sky pregnant
with possible snow. But still there
was light enough to see. The carpenter
must have covered the hole in the roof
to keep the attic dry.

The mason turned to his work. He filled
the tub part full of cement and sand
and began, with measured care, to add
water and blend and mix.

He worked hard against the brittle cold.
By mid-afternoon he opened the attic door
and climbed the stairs to discover
why he had not been able to see the sky.

The carpenter had missed the mark,
had cut the final hole in the roof
on the opposite side of the ridgepole
from where the chimney sat.

Undaunted, the mason mixed strong mortar
and with a smile (and his tongue clipped
between his teeth at the corner of his mouth),
he leaned the chimney to the left,
course by offset course,
and eased it through the crosscut hole.

The next morning, in a light snow,
he raised it high above the roof and joined
it to the sky, capping it with a double
rim of edge-turned brick.

I have come now, a stranger, all these
years after. Standing in the stairwell,
my eye follows the leaning line
of bricks that holds and marks the path
of smoke that curves into a winter
afternoon. In the dim light of a dormer
window we share a laugh—that mason,
that carpenter, and me, each of us aware
of a craftsman's awesome vulnerability,
his perpetual need for accepting friends,
past and present.

And the memory of our laughter, as it
always has, will wait in darkness
with a timeless patience to bond us one day
to another stranger.

—CHARLES E. COCKELREAS